TRACERS

A Mermaid Dramabook

 HILL AND WANG · NEW YORK

A division of Farrar, Straus and Giroux

TRACERS

A play conceived by JOHN DiFUSCO

written by the original cast:

VINCENT CARISTI

RICHARD CHAVES

JOHN DiFUSCO

ERIC E. EMERSON

RICK GALLAVAN

MERLIN MARSTON

HARRY STEPHENS

with SHELDON LETTICH

*Library of Congress Cataloging-in-Publication Data
Main entry under title:
Tracers: a play.
(A Mermaid dramabook)
1. Vietnamese Conflict, 1961–1979—Drama.
I. DiFusco, John. II. Caristi, Vincent.
PS3570.R2 1986 812'.54 86-295*

Dedicated to
the 59,000 who missed the Freedom Bird

The History of TRACERS

Tracers was conceived by John DiFusco and created by a group of actors—Vincent Caristi, Richard Chaves, Eric E. Emerson, Rick Gallavan, Merlin Marston, Harry Stephens, and John DiFusco—and one writer, Sheldon Lettich, all of whom are Vietnam veterans. It is based on their personal experiences. In April 1980, DiFusco organized the group and led workshops toward the creation of a play. The workshops consisted of a variety of techniques: personal improvisation, rap sessions, psychodrama, physical work, and ensemble work, to name a few. Sheldon Lettich was a frequent participant and did some writing, as well as transcriptions of improvisations, which were then edited by him and DiFusco.

The first three months of work were conducted in complete privacy. A play seemed to be developing, and a work-in-progress performance was given at the Odyssey Theatre in Los Angeles on July 4, 1980. The response from an invited audience was encouraging, so the workshops resumed and an assistant director, Deborah Barylski, was recruited. Finally, in October 1980, DiFusco completed the overall structure of the play, i.e., scene order, music and sound design, choreography, and final editing.

The play opened on October 17, 1980, at the Odyssey Theatre. It was a critical success and ran for nine months, during which it was awarded the Drama-Logue Critics' Award for Direction and the Los Angeles Drama Critics' Award for Ensemble Performance. *Tracers* was next produced by the Steppenwolf Theatre Company of Chicago in January 1984, and was awarded the 1984 Joseph Jefferson Award for Best Ensemble Performance. The play made its New York debut at the Public Theatre. Directed by DiFusco, it featured two members of the original Los Angeles cast, Vincent Caristi and Richard Chaves. The production was critically acclaimed, and played to capacity houses for six months. DiFusco was awarded the 1985 Drama Desk Award for Sound and Music Design, and Chaves received the *Theatre World* Award for Outstanding New Talent. In August 1985, the play was presented at the Royal Court Theatre in London.

Originally presented at the Odyssey Theatre in Los Angeles, produced by Ron Sossi and Lupe Vargas, October 17, 1980, through July 6, 1981.

PROFESSOR	Harry Stephens
SERGEANT WILLIAMS/HABU	Eric E. Emerson
BABY SAN	Vincent Caristi
DINKY DAU	Richard Chaves
DOC	John DiFusco
LITTLE JOHN	Merlin Marston
SCOOTER	Rick Gallavan

Directed by John DiFusco. *Assistant director:* Deborah Barylski

Presented by the Steppenwolf Theatre Company, Chicago, January 24 through April 7, 1984.

PROFESSOR	Tom Irwin
SERGEANT WILLIAMS	Dennis Farina
BABY SAN	Alan Wilder
DINKY DAU	Terry Kinney
HABU	Greg Williams
DOC	Will Zahrn
LITTLE JOHN	Afram Bill Williams
SCOOTER	Gary Cole

Directed by Gary Sinise

Presented by the Vietnam Veterans Ensemble Theatre Company, Thomas Bird, Artistic Director, at the New York Shakespeare Festival's Public Theatre, Joseph Papp, Producer, January 9 through July 7, 1985.

PROFESSOR	R. J. Bonds
SERGEANT WILLIAMS	J. Kenneth Campbell
BABY SAN	Vincent Caristi
DINKY DAU	Richard Chaves
HABU	Anthony Chisholm
DOC	Josh Cruze
LITTLE JOHN	Brian Delate
SCOOTER	Jim Tracy

Directed by John DiFusco. *Scenery by* John Falabella. *Costumes by* David Navarro Velasquez. *Lighting by* Terry Wuthrich. *Dramaturgy by* David Berry. *Production Stage Manager:* Michael Chambers

Presented by the Royal Court Theatre Upstairs in London in collaboration with the New York Shakespeare Festival, Joseph Papp, Producer, and the Vietnam Veterans Ensemble Theatre Company, Thomas Bird, Artistic Director, August 6 through September 7, 1985.

PROFESSOR	R. J. Bonds
SERGEANT WILLIAMS	Eric E. Emerson
BABY SAN	Vincent Caristi
DINKY DAU	Richard Chaves
HABU	Anthony Chisholm
DOC	Josh Cruze
LITTLE JOHN	Brian Delate
SCOOTER	Rick Gallavan

Directed by John DiFusco

*"Make the first two or three rounds tracers.
That way, when you see two red streaks in a row,
you know you're runnin' outta ammo."*

TRACERS

ACT ONE

Photo © 1986 John Haynes of the Royal Court Theatre production in London (l to r): Anthony Chisholm, R. J. Bonds, Vincent Caristi, Josh Cruze, Richard Chaves, Rick Gallavan, and Brian Delate

The play is performed with fragmented costuming (when in Vietnam, a fatigue shirt and a bush hat suffice; "Tracers," and other stateside scenes should be performed in civvies) and a minimum of props, except for six M—16s, which are visible in a rack onstage.

Set: Simple platforms and camouflaged backdrop.

Time: Fluctuates between 1980s, just after the war, and during the war.

Prologue

Whispered in darkness by the ensemble. The following lines alternate from one actor to another.

ENSEMBLE: Someone told me you're a vet!
Someone told me you had a gun.
You killed people?
You were only nineteen?
You volunteered?
You're bullshitting me.
Oh, you're one of the lucky ones who made it back.

I'm sorry.

I suppose you don't want to talk about it?

Yeah, we saw that on TV.

How was the heat?

How was the rain?

How were the women?

How was Bob Hope?

How does it feel to kill somebody?

You were a pawn.

You were a hero.

You were stupid, you should have gone to Canada.

You were there?

You were there?

You were there?

You were there?

You were there?

You were there?

FADE-IN MUSIC: *"Walkin' on a Thin Line" by Huey Lewis and the News.*

Walkin' on a Thin Line

Lights up on first vocal, "Walkin' on a Thin Line" by Huey Lewis and the News. A choreographed ensemble dance ensues, which is both an interpretation of the song and a statement of camaraderie.

Home from the War—The First Tracers

Music and lights cross-fade. Bruce Springsteen's "Shut Out the Light" underscores the beginning and end of each of the following monologues. The actors isolated on stage change to sixties' civilian clothing.

SCOOTER: I keep havin' this dream about a trip I'm goin' on. I board a plane for Europe, but I always end up in Vietnam. I look down from the plane, and I can see a lot of shit goin' on below. I get off the plane, and then I can't find my unit. I meet other GIs on the road. I ask them about my unit. But they just give me bullshit answers. I dive into a bunker. And Little John is sittin' there. He's covered with blood and he's been cryin'. I ask him what he's doin' there, and why he isn't buried. He just starts laughin' and floats right up into my face and he says, "You don't think I know I'm dead? I want you to know somethin', man, I'm pissed off, I don't get to go home." We get hit with a ground attack. I see the VC shoot Little John, and I shoot two fuckin' VC. But in my dream nobody dies. Everybody just gets up and we all walk off—together.

(Music up. Lights cross-fade)

LITTLE JOHN *(Examining the sores on his skin)*: Lately I get so fucking frustrated, I just wanna smash things. I've been punching in doors, windows, mirrors. Sometimes I'll be at a party. I'll listen to a couple of people talking. For no reason at all, I feel like walking up to them and smashing them right in the face. I don't want to hurt anybody anymore. And these sores. I feel like a freak. Fuck it, man, fuck it.

(Music up. Lights cross-fade)

BABY SAN: I'm packin' my things. I hear my folks. They're talkin' about me again. Why doesn't he go to school? Why doesn't he get a job? What's he doin' comin' home so late for? *(He screams)* "I got to get out of here." "So go," he says. "Get an apartment in Manhattan," he says. Like that's some kinda big fuckin' deal. I says, "Hey, Pop, a year in Vietnam, *that's* a big fuckin' deal! What do you want? Do you want me to be a computer operator? Get married, have a couple of kids, live in the suburbs? For who? For you? *I* was happenin' there. It was a party."

(Music up. Lights cross-fade) DINKY DAU *enters slowly, in a wheelchair)*

DINKY DAU: I was cruising down the boardwalk in Venice Beach and this Amazon Queen in a one-piece string walks right in front of me. Wham! I slammed on the brakes. Whoa, I'm sorry. Hey, you wanna dance? Are you fuckin' crazy, she says to me, and runs over to her boyfriend, a Charles Atlas look-alike. Fuckin' jack-off. Fuck her and my ex-wife. Those kind of women, they don't understand. You know, some of them can't even look at me, they all think I'm crazy. But I've been tryin' to straighten myself out and get off the skag. Maybe they're right; I am boo coo dinky dau. I don't want to need a woman, but I do. Now Vietnamese women, they were different. Appearances didn't matter to them. They knew the value of a touch, or just a smile. It was special to them. They made me feel special. They weren't whores—I know what you're thinking, but they weren't. They were women. Very special women.

(Music up. LITTLE JOHN *walks up behind him and pushes him offstage. Lights cross-fade)*

HABU: April 1968, the West Side of Chicago. Hot, humid, buildings burnin', teargas, and bullets. Another war goin' on. I had to get outta Garfield. So I got into my red Camaro, bought with blood money. Eisenhower to Lake Shore Drive, headin' south, I see a red light, I run it. I run another one. Goin' faster and faster. Soldier Field, red light, run it. Goin' faster and faster. Thirty-fifth Street, the projects—headin' south, speedometer risin', heart poundin', I keep runnin' red lights, red lights streakin' across my mind, it's a solid line of bright red. When you load your magazines, make the first two or three rounds tracers. That way when you see two or three red streaks in a row, you know you're runnin' out of ammo . . . time to reload.

(Music up. Lights cross-fade)

THE PROFESSOR: I was sitting in my apartment, trying to meditate. Suddenly I felt myself go numb. My mind separating from my body. The room—my environment— everything around me was moving up and away from me. I couldn't feel myself sitting on the floor. My heart was pounding rapidly, pressing against my chest. I could feel the veins in my neck and my temples throbbing. I thought maybe I was having a heart attack! *(Stands, gasping for air. Gets up and starts pacing)* I couldn't feel myself walking on the floor! I thought, Maybe I'll call someone, but who? What would I say? Ah, fuck, I couldn't dial the phone. I was losing control. I thought I was going insane. All I knew was, I was scared. No, this couldn't have anything to do with Vietnam. But I do remember certain places, and certain people's faces . . .

(Fade to black)

Saigon List

(Whispered in blackout, each actor alternating lines)

ENSEMBLE: Doc. Professor. Dinky Dau. Little John. Baby San. Habu. Scooter. Saigon. Da Nang. Phu Cat. Camranh Bay. The 'Nam. The world. Hootch. Bunker. Sandbags. Concertina wire. Gook. Slope. Dink. Victor Charles. November Victor alpha. Skivvy girls. I souvenir you, GI. Boom-boom. Numbah-fuckin' one. I trade you carton of Salems. I love you too much, GI. Girlsan. Boysan. Mamasan. Papasan. Babysan.

(Lights up. Remainder of list is choreographed in ritualistic style)

ENSEMBLE: La dai, motherfucker! Mos skosh! Deedee mau! I kinda fuckin' doubt it. There it is, GI. I can't feel my legs. Sorry 'bout that shit. Dog tags. He's dead. Wasted. KIA. Head wound. Stomach wound. A fuckin' suckin' chest wound. Medavac. Dustoff. Clear to fire in any direction. I have zero two kilo India alphas. Hueys. Chinooks. Cobra gunships. "Freedom Bird"! Steam an' cream. Ham an' motherfuckers. Beans an' dicks. Lurps. Heat tabs. Boo coo. Tee tee. The bush. The boonies. In the rear. With the gear. And the beer. Smoke. Skag. Speed. Com sai. If it's green, it's good. If it ain't green, paint it.

(One by one, the actors fall into military formation)

ENSEMBLE: Lifers. Short-timers. I ain't short, I'm next. I ain't next, I'm gone. Incoming! Helmet. Flak jacket. Poncho liner. Bolt firing pin. Trigger housing group. Check your fields of fire. Ready on the right. Ready on the left. Fire the one-oh-six! Atten-hut! *(Marching and singing)* Right shoulder—arms! Yo' lef', yo' lef, yo' left, right lef'. If I die in a combat zone/Box me up and send me home. Sound off . . . one, two . . . Sound off . . . three, four . . . Bring it on down. One two three four. One two three four!

(The following lines are performed in a round. One by one the actors address the audience, breaking the military formation. Each actor repeats the line)

ENSEMBLE: You're all going to Vietnam; if you don't pay attention, you're gonna die.

(Evolve to marching sounds. Tableau of actors about to meet each other, hand-shaking, etc.)

Day One

Break tableau with ad libs of "What's your name?" "Where are you from?" etc. Cut off by drill instructor SERGEANT WILLIAMS's *line, beginning offstage. The tempo of his speech is rapid-fire.*

WILLIAMS: Find yourselves a pair of yellow footprints, maggots.

OTHERS: Uh, oh. . . . what was that?

WILLIAMS: A pair of yellow footprints, maggots!

OTHERS *(Ad libs)*: I think that's our ID. That's DI, etc. *(All search for yellow footprints to stand on)*

WILLIAMS: I said find yourselves a pair of yellow footprints. By the time I get down there, maggots had better have gotten rid of their cigarettes, their goddamn candy, their goddamn soda pop, their goddamn fuck books. They had best be standin' on that pair of yellow footprints at the position of goddamn attention! *(By this time he is onstage. He alternates between addressing the audience and addressing the actors. He walks up and down the line of men)* The position of attention means: feet at a forty-five-degree angle, thumbs along the seams of trousers, stomach in, chest out, shoulders back, chin in, head and eyes locked straight to the front! While maggots are at attention, they will not talk, they will not eye-fuck the area, they will listen to me and only me! From this day forth, the first word out of a maggot's mouth is "Sir," the last word out of a maggot's mouth is "Sir." Do maggots understand me?

OTHERS: Sir, yes, sir.

WILLIAMS: Get it together, maggots!

OTHERS: Sir, yes, sir.

WILLIAMS: Louder!

OTHERS: Sir, yes, sir.

WILLIAMS: I got a ninety-five-year-old grandmother that talks louder than that. Again!

OTHERS: *Sir, yes, sir!!!*

WILLIAMS: My name is Drill Instructor Sergeant Williams. For the next nine weeks, I will be your mother, your father, your sister, your brother, your aunt, your uncle, your cousin, your niece, your goddamn girlfriend—but don't fuck with me!!! *(SCOOTER snickers)* Maggots will soon begin to think I am God. Maggots will not be far from wrong. *(He grabs SCOOTER by the throat)* Does the maggot think it heard something funny?

SCOOTER: Well, you see, sir, I thought it was funny . . .

WILLIAMS: Eyes?! Those goddamn slimy fuckin' peepers in your fuckin' forehead are fuckin' eyes! This slimy piece of whale shit in front of me is a goddamn maggot! Does the maggot understand this?

SCOOTER: Sir, yes, sir!

WILLIAMS: Good. Let's make sure the maggot does not forget, shall we? Get down! Push-ups, maggots, one hundred repetitions. Ready, exercise. *(SCOOTER begins doing push-ups)* That's right, maggot, you do them till my dick gets hard. Do I have any other maggots think something I have said is funny? Look to the left of you, maggots! Now look to the right of you, maggots. Now look at the maggot directly in front of you or directly behind you, maggots . . . Look to the front! Next time any of you maggots thinks something I say is funny, best think over what I'm about to say.

In just a few short months, one of the maggots you just looked at will be a *dead* maggot! Now some of you maggots are beginning to think the chemical fertilizer has hit the ventilation system. You're beginning to wish you were back on the block, diddly-boppin' around, eye-fuckin' the area, chasin' yourselves some round-eyed pussy. Well, forget it! Skatin' time for maggots is done! In just a few short months, any of you maggots happens to make it through my basic training program *alive* will find his sorry ass shipped to the republic of South Vietnam. Maggots, this place will seem like a goddamn Sunday-school picnic compared to the world of hurt you will find in the jungle. *(To* DINKY DAU*)* Maggot, I'm not boring you, am I?

DINKY DAU: Sir, no, sir!

WILLIAMS: You wish you were back on the block with your girlfriend, Little Sally Rottencrotch, don't you, maggot?!

DINKY DAU: Sir, no, sir!

WILLIAMS: That's real good, maggot, because as soon as you walked out that front door, your best buddy came in through the back door. Jody's humpin' Sally right now; he's playin' with her titties, suckin' on her clitty, and makin' her come. So you do not have to worry about Sally no more, she will not get bored. And, maggot, neither will you. Get up there. Side-straddle hops—five hundred repetitions. Ready. Exercise! *(*DINKY DAU *is confused)* Jumpin' jacks, you asshole! *(*DINKY DAU *begins doing jumping jacks)* That's right, maggot. You do 'em until I get tired. *(Pause)* Maggots, over in the republic of South Vietnam, we got tall green elephant grass. Maggots what ain't got their shit together in one itsy-bitsy, little bag go over to the republic of South Vietnam and get lost in that tall green elephant grass. Now, Luke the Gook, Link the Chink, and Charlie Cong like to hide in that tall green elephant grass and they *love* to kill maggots. Now, I, Drill Instructor Sergeant Williams, do not like Luke the Gook, Link the Chink, or Charlie Cong. I do not like them killin' my maggots. So if I got any maggots what ain't got their shit together in one itsy-bitsy, tiny little bag, I would rather kill them myself. And I just might do that. You maggots ain't got but nine weeks to get your heads and asses wired together, or for sure you are gonna die—every swingin' dick one of you. *(To the* PROFESSOR*)* Maggot, *you* are a *hippie*.

PROFESSOR: Sir, no, sir!

WILLIAMS: You're some kind of goddamn flower child, ain't you, maggot?

PROFESSOR: Sir, no, sir!

WILLIAMS: You think your Uncle Sam is gonna send your sorry ass to war so you can lie in the Vietnam sun, smokin' all that good Vietnamese dope, listenin' to that goddamn psychedelic rock 'n' roll, don't you?

PROFESSOR: Sir, no, sir!

WILLIAMS: Well, just what the fuck are you doing here, flower child?

PROFESSOR *(Flustered)*: Sir . . . they . . .

WILLIAMS: Are you gonna make me wait for an answer, flower child?

PROFESSOR: Sir, the maggot does not know, sir!

WILLIAMS: What? The maggot does not know, sir? Oh wow, goddamn it, flower child; well, maybe you better take a break and think about it for a while. Get down! *(PROFESSOR lies face down)* Get up on your elbows and toes, flower child! *(He gets up on elbows and toes)* That's it, flower child, you lie there and you meditate . . . you meditate on what Luke the Gook's gonna do to your sorry ass when he's got an AK–47 up your nose and you tell him, "Peace, love, happiness, dope."

(WILLIAMS turns on HABU, who has a copy of Eldridge Cleaver's Soul on Ice *in his pocket or hand.* HABU *wears shades and possibly a dashiki)*

WILLIAMS: Hey, maggot, I thought I told you to get rid of your goddamn fuck books.

HABU: Sir, it's not a fuck book, sir.

WILLIAMS: Then what the fuck is it, diddly-boppin' motherfucker? *(He grabs the book and reads the cover)* Soul on Ice! Eldridge Cleaver. Have I got me a militant? I got me a fuckin' Black Panther or some shit here. *(Gets in his face)* Lose the dark glasses, soul brother. You in the real world now. *(HABU removes them slowly)* Maggot, what fuckin' color are you?

HABU: Sir, black, sir.

WILLIAMS: Guess again, maggot.

HABU: Sir, brown, sir.

WILLIAMS: That's twice you wrong, maggot. You wanna go for strike three?

HABU: Sir, no, sir.

WILLIAMS: Get down on your back, maggot. (HABU *does*) Knees up, maggot. Now you do sit-ups till your ass turns green, maggot. (HABU *starts doing sit-ups.* WILLIAMS *addresses the group*) Maggots, I ain't got no black maggots. I ain't got no white maggots. I ain't got no red or yellow or brown maggots. All my maggots are green. Only color maggots are issued in is green. You got that?!

ALL: Sir, yes, sir.

SCOOTER: Sir.

WILLIAMS: Speak, maggot.

SCOOTER: Sir, the maggot requests permission to stand up, sir.

WILLIAMS: Aw, is the maggot gettin' tired?

SCOOTER: Sir, yes, sir!

WILLIAMS: Is the maggot gonna fall asleep on Drill Instructor Sergeant Williams?

SCOOTER: Sir, no, sir!

WILLIAMS: Damn right you're not! Get up! Get over there. You see what your buddy's doin' over there? *(He points to* DINKY DAU *doing jumping jacks)*

SCOOTER: Sir, yes, sir.

WILLIAMS: Join him!

*(*SCOOTER *begins doing jumping jacks)*

WILLIAMS: That's right, maggot, I wanna make good and goddamn sure you do not fall asleep on me. *(To* PROFESSOR*)* Flower child!

PROFESSOR: Sir, yes, sir?

WILLIAMS: You ain't gettin' tired on me also, are you?

PROFESSOR *(Straining)*: Sir, no, sir!

WILLIAMS: You're a liar, flower child! Push-ups—five hundred—thousand of them. Ready. Exercise.

*(*PROFESSOR *begins doing push-ups.* WILLIAMS *crosses to* LITTLE JOHN*)*

WILLIAMS: Goddamn, you one big fuckin' maggot, ain't you? Goddamn it, maggot, how come you ain't out playin' football someplace, maggot? How come you didn't get no bullshit deferment like Joe Namath and the rest of those goddamn candy-ass fuckin' football players? Speak!

LITTLE JOHN: Sir, the maggot wants to fight for his country, sir!

WILLIAMS: Say again.

LITTLE JOHN: Sir, the maggot wants to fight for his country, sir!

WILLIAMS: Have I got me a maggot what thinks it's John-fuckin'-Wayne? Gimme a John-fuckin'-Wayne yell, maggot!

LITTLE JOHN: Move out, pilgrim!

WILLIAMS: Louder, maggot. I want Ho Chi Minh to hear you so he knows you comin' to kick his ass. Motivate me!

LITTLE JOHN: I said, Move out, pilgrim!!

WILLIAMS: Goddamn it, we better find you some enemy to kill real soon, hadn't we? Get down. Now you low-crawl around my basic trainin' formation, and as soon as you spot some enemy, you let me know. You got that?

(LITTLE JOHN *crawls around the basic training formation.* BABY SAN *looks at* WILLIAMS. WILLIAMS *catches him*)

WILLIAMS (*To* BABY SAN): Are you queer for my gear, you sawed-off, cross-eyed abortion of the afterbirth of a syphilitic whore? I told you to lock your head and eyes straight to the front, didn't I?

BABY SAN: Sir, yes, sir!

WILLIAMS: Goddamn right I did. Goddamn, you're one little tiny fuckin' maggot, ain't you?

BABY SAN: Sir, yes, sir.

WILLIAMS: Goddamn it, little maggot, don't you know we got a height requirement? Were you wearing elevator shoes when you talked to your goddamn recruiter?

BABY SAN: Sir, I . . .

WILLIAMS: Speak, maggot!

BABY SAN: Sir . . .

WILLIAMS: Enlighten me!

BABY SAN *(Feebly)*: Well, you see, sir, I was drafted, sir.

(WILLIAMS *points to the floor.* BABY SAN *gets down ready to do push-ups*)

WILLIAMS: No, no, no—on your back, you slimy, scuzzy, scum-bag, civilian, fuckin' draftee. On your back!

BABY SAN: Sir, yes, sir.

WILLIAMS: Goddamn it, Uncle Sam stomped down out of the sky and squashed your young ass to the ground, didn't he?

BABY SAN: Sir, yes, sir.

WILLIAMS: You're one squashed maggot, aren't you?

BABY SAN: Sir, yes, sir.

WILLIAMS: You know what a squashed maggot looks like?

BABY SAN: Sir, no, sir.

WILLIAMS: It looks like a dying fuckin' cockroach maggot. You know what a dying cockroach looks like?

BABY SAN: Sir, no, sir.

WILLIAMS: Well, I will instruct you. Get your legs up in the air.

BABY SAN (*Follows* WILLIAMS's *every instruction*): Sir, yes, sir.

WILLIAMS: Get your arms up in the air.

BABY SAN: Sir, yes, sir.

WILLIAMS: Now wave them the fuck around. Say, "Sir, I am a dying fuckin' cockroach, sir."

BABY SAN: Sir, I am a dying fuckin' cockroach, sir.

(BABY SAN *repeats this line until told to shut up.* WILLIAMS *turns to audience*)

WILLIAMS: Goddamn it, slimy, scuzzy, scum-bag, civilian fuckin' draftees. What kind of shit are they unloading on my poor tired old ass? This is the sorriest herd of maggots they ever dumped on me. Just look at them! (WILLIAMS *turns to* SCOOTER, *who has stopped exercising*) Did somebody tell you to stop?!

SCOOTER: Sir, no, sir.

WILLIAMS: Goddamn right they didn't.

BABY SAN: Sir, I'm a dying fuckin' cock . . .

WILLIAMS: Cockroach?

BABY SAN: Sir, yes, sir?

WILLIAMS: Shut the fuck up.

BABY SAN: Sir, yes, sir.

WILLIAMS: Goddamn it, I had a better set of toy soldiers when I was five years old. I would like to send this whole slimy herd back to their mommies. I would like to, but I cannot. I am stuck with them, and I am good and right-eously pissed! You maggots hear that?! Drill Instructor Sergeant Williams is good and righteously pissed, his maggots are in a world of deep, deep shit! I gotta do something to relieve the fuckin' frustration. Maggots, find yourselves a pair of yellow footprints . . . Ready, move! (*All frantically scramble into formation, except the* PROFESSOR. WILLIAMS *to* PROFESSOR) Get back. This doped-up hippie was too fuckin' slow, maggots, and now you're all dead. (*All scramble back, resume their exercises*) When I say "Move!" it is greased-fuckin' lightning time. Now, look at a pair of yellow footprints—scope them out—get ready—move! *(All scramble into formation like greased lightning)* Better. Now, maggots, Drill Instructor Sergeant Williams has got to do something to relieve the fuckin' frustration. So I am gonna tell you what he is gonna do. He's gonna take this slimy fuckin' herd over to the goddamn barbershop. He's gonna watch them lose all their excessive civilian hair—every little tiny bit of it. He's gonna take them over to the supply. Get rid of this filthy, slimy, disgusting, colorful, civilian clothing—get them some nice clean green uniforms to play in instead. This will make Drill Instructor Sergeant Williams slightly happy. Conceivably, it could make him smile. Maggots want him to smile, don't they?

ALL: Sir, yes, sir.

WILLIAMS: Goddamn right you do. Turn to your left, herd.

(All turn left except for SCOOTER, *who turns right)*

WILLIAMS: Your military left, you stupid fuckin' shithead! Get your goddamn left arms up in the goddamn air: ready—move! *(All raise their left arms)* Good guess. I am good and righteously pleased to see that all my maggots are equipped with their left arms on the same goddamn side of their goddamn bodies. Now, get asshole to belly button. I said, get asshole to belly button. If I see any space between you and the man in front of you, I'll reach in and knock your dick stiff. Now, when I say move, you will lower your left arm—put it on the left shoulder of the maggot directly in front of you—all 'cept my biggest fuckin' maggot—you ain't got no left shoulder in front of you, do you?

LITTLE JOHN: Sir, no, sir.

WILLIAMS: Do you see that goddamn barbershop pole?

LITTLE JOHN: Sir, yes, sir!

WILLIAMS: When I say move, you will lower your arm and follow your left thumb till it touches that goddamn barbershop pole, got that?

LITTLE JOHN: Sir, yes, sir.

WILLIAMS: Goddamn right you do. Ready—move! *(All quickly lower their arms)* Giddyup, herd! *(They hesitatingly begin moving forward)* Giddyup, move! Move! *(They begin shuffling faster)* Hurry up! Move! Move! *(They run offstage)* You got three seconds to get there and two of 'em are already up.

Day One Epilogue

Lights cross-fade to spot on WILLIAMS, *who addresses the audience.*

WILLIAMS: The Union of Soviet Socialist Republics trains its infantry for eighteen months. We train ours for eighteen weeks. Charlie Cong has been at it for twenty-six years. We issue them the most sophisticated equipment in the world, but we do not teach them how to use it. We commit them to the combat zone in units so large that their support facilities become targets for insurgents. They are now eighteen and nineteen years old. Before they are twenty-one, nearly half of them will be killed or wounded.

With a two-year draft, we send out amateurs to play against pros in a game for keeps. Ten percent should not even be here. Eighty percent are targets; we have no time to train them to be more. Ten percent are fighters. One in a hundred may become a warrior. I must seek him out. I must come down heavy on him. Upon him the success or failure of our present conflict lies. Ten percent are fighters. One in one hundred is a warrior. Eighty percent are targets.

(He comes to attention, salutes, does a right face, and exits)

Sense of Judgment

Music up: "Fixin' to Die Rag" by Country Joe and the Fish, mixed with Vietnamese music and chopper sound effects. BABY SAN enters. He dons fatigue shirt, takes weapon, examines it, moves about the stage, begins to look at imaginary bodies on stage floor. He kicks at a body and begins to pillage it. He pulls something from it.

BABY SAN: Look at this fuckin' belt buckle, Little John. *(He notices audience for the first time and begins to deliver the following to them)* I lost my sense of judgment yesterday. I killed someone. Who? I don't know, we've never met. You think you have to know someone to kill them. After all, it's just you and him, and it's a very important part of both of your lives. But I'm still here. Where? In the land of Buddha—and banyan trees, and Cao Dai temples and South China seas. Hey, papasan, I'll have another peppermint schnapps, please. Gee, isn't Saigon beautiful?! I feel like I'm in Paris. This is an outdoor café. Those are boulevards, statues, taxicabs, and barbed wire. I lost my sense of judgment yesterday, I traded two cartons of Salem cigarettes for something I should have traded one for. Now the guys are laughing at me. But it's good pot, though. And that little mamasan's face, so brown, so sincere. "Chao, babysan, mon yoi, ong mua den to toi, cho ong so mot com sai. You buy from me, I give you number-one com sai." Her? No, she's not humping rockets for the VC. Hey, do you think I killed her baby? I lost my sense of judgment yesterday. You see, I sat down in my bunker and I wrote a letter to my girlfriend and I said, "Julie, I don't think that I love you anymore." She hasn't written me back since. Since I only told the truth. And the truth is . . . I don't know. I want to wake up now, I would like to go home now. You see, we live in bunkers here and we carry M–16s. She's nineteen, too. She goes to college. She doesn't even know what a mortar round sounds like. A couple of weeks ago I got a letter from her. She wants my opinion on a wedding dress. *(Laughs)* I lost my sense of judgment yesterday, and Brooklyn seems like a world away.

(Vietnamese music up. Lights cross-fade as he exits)

Initiation

Vietnamese music up. DINKY DAU *and* SCOOTER *enter simultaneously from different sides of stage. They exchange hellos.* SCOOTER *goes to the M–16s and quietly checks his out.* DINKY DAU *carries an Instamatic camera. He sees some imaginary Vietnamese women walking, approaches them by moving toward the audience, and begins to snap pictures of them.*

26

DINKY DAU: Hey, mamasan, mamasan, over here. How 'bout if I take a picture of you. *(Pause)* Aw, hey, c'mon, it's just a camera. Hey, mamasan, where you goin'? Hey, come back here—I'm not gonna hurt you. *(To* SCOOTER*)* Hey, Scooter, what the hell is wrong with them? Why'd they run away from me like that?

SCOOTER: Those mamasans are afraid of your camera, Dinky Dau. They think it's got the evil eye in it.

DINKY DAU: Oh yeah. Well, let me take a picture of you, then, Scooter.

SCOOTER: Sure.

*(*SCOOTER *poses with his M–16 in one hand, flashing the peace sign with the other.* DINKY DAU *snaps photo)*

DINKY DAU: Here, you take one of me.

*(*DINKY DAU *hands* SCOOTER *the camera. He poses,* SCOOTER *raises the camera . . . Loud explosion. He scrambles to one side of the stage, crouches down holding his hands over his head, screaming)* Incoming! Incoming!

(Explosion stops. SCOOTER *snaps picture of* DINKY DAU*)*

SCOOTER: Outgoing.

DINKY DAU: Was that Bridge Security firing the one-oh-six? Jesus Christ, Scooter, I can't get used to this incoming/outgoing shit.

SCOOTER: Dinky Dau, relax. You're making everybody nervous. And the next time those mamasans run away from you like that and you want them to come back, just say, "La dai, gook."

DINKY DAU (*Nervously*): La dai, gook?

SCOOTER: Yeah, and if you want 'em to get the fuck away from you, just say, "Deedee mau, dink."

DINKY DAU (*Nervously*): Deedee mau, dink?

SCOOTER: And most important of all, if you want a piece of ass, just say, "Hey, mamasan, you give me number-one boom-boom."

DINKY DAU: Number-one boom-boom?

SCOOTER: Right. Don't ask for number ten, 'cause that's what you'll get. Ask for number one. And don't go gettin' attached to these people. They ain't nothin' but zipper-headed, rice-eatin', war-losin', gook motherfuckers.

DINKY DAU (*Having trouble saying it*): Zipper-headed . . . war-losin' . . .

(HABU *enters*, LITTLE JOHN *following behind*)

HABU: Zipper-headed, rice-eatin', war-losin', gook motherfuckers. (*To* SCOOTER) Scooter, you teachin' him all them big words already?

SCOOTER: Sure, Habu. He almost knows the difference between incoming and outgoing.

HABU: Dinky Dau, good for you.

(*The* PROFESSOR *enters*)

DINKY DAU: I'm learnin'.

PROFESSOR: The first step toward a promising career.

LITTLE JOHN: And get you some towels to wrap those magazines in.

DINKY DAU: Habu, I tried to get some towels from Supply the other day, and the supply sergeant said they're all out of 'em.

PROFESSOR (*Laughs*): Supply!

(*All ad-lib: "Oh, they were all out," etc. Laughs*)

HABU: You tried to get 'em from *Supply*? That's real good, Dinky Dau. That's number-fuckin'-one.

SCOOTER: Hey, man, you want anything from Supply, you gotta sneak in and steal it when they ain't lookin'.

PROFESSOR: They are perpetually out of everything.

DINKY DAU: Uh, I don't mean to sound like a stupid shit or nothin'.

PROFESSOR: Take it easy, Dinky Dau.

HABU: Dinky Dau, we're not tryin' to give you a hard time. We're just tryin' to explain things to you the way they are out here—you gotta pacify this shit.

DINKY DAU: I'll steal myself some towels.

HABU: Numbah-fuckin' one.

SCOOTER (*Looking offstage*): Hey, check out this dude.

(*Enter* BABY SAN *wearing a helmet and carrying a full pack, with an M–16 slung over his shoulder. He trips over himself, nervously looks around the stage*)

BABY SAN: Hey, you guys from the Second Platoon that's goin' out on this here patrol?

PROFESSOR: Can we lie?

HABU: Who wants to know?

BABY SAN: I do. My name's Kris.

LITTLE JOHN: Are you the guy that's supposed to replace Falcon?

BABY SAN: I dunno, this guy named Staff Sergeant Williams told me I was supposed to come over here . . .

HABU: Williams, you motherfucker!

(Others ad-lib negative remarks about WILLIAMS*)*

BABY SAN: Uh, he said I was supposed to go out on patrol with you guys.

HABU: Well, why don't you *deedee mau mos stosk ricky-tick* up that hill and you find Staff Sergeant Williams and tell him that I just got me an FNG last week and I don't need me another one.

BABY SAN: What's an FNG?

LITTLE JOHN: It's a fuckin' new guy.

BABY SAN: New, I ain't new—I've been in-country six months.

LITTLE JOHN: You've had a sling on your rifle for six fuckin' months?

HABU: All right, fuck it. Who wants Baby San here?

(All ad-lib negative answers: "I had the last one," etc.)

LITTLE JOHN: I'll take him, Habu.

*(*BABY SAN *seats himself next to* LITTLE JOHN*)*

BABY SAN: Thanks, man. *(Pause)* By the way, like I said, my name is Kris.

HABU: Well, Kris, it's Baby San now. That's your team leader, Little John, that's Scooter, that's the Professor, that's our other newby, we call it Dinky Dau, and you can call me Habu.

BABY SAN: Tabu? Like the perfume? *(He laughs to himself)*

HABU: Baby San, don't fuck with me. Little John, you do me one big favor . . .

LITTLE JOHN: I'll keep an eye on him, Habu.

(HABU *takes out a grid map, places it in the center of the group. All gather around map)*

HABU: Okay, listen up. We're right here. We'll be goin' out through the wire and down along this ridge line. Come back over this ridge line, this hook in the river is our first check point. *(Points to it)*

(BABY SAN *looks out toward audience)*

SCOOTER: You wanna listen up here, Baby San?

HABU: Take my word for it, Baby San, you cannot see it from here. *(He continues)* This hook in the river. That's inside a free-fire zone. That means, we see anything, we hear anything, we so much as smell anything, we ain't gonna ask it no questions. We're just gonna do it. Now, are you two newbys perfectly clear on that?

DINKY DAU: I got it, Habu.

BABY SAN: Uh, Corporal . . .

HABU: *(Direct and intense)*: Ha-bu.

BABY SAN: Uh, Ha-bu . . . are you, uh, expectin' any action out there?

SCOOTER: No, Baby San, we're just goin' out to set up for the Bob Hope Show.

HABU: Scooter, don't tell him that. Baby San, just how long did you say you've been in-country?

BABY SAN: Six months.

LITTLE JOHN: That's a mighty shiny belt buckle, Baby San. Just how many patrols have you been out on?

BABY SAN: This is my first patrol.

(All express indignation, mutter about WILLIAMS, etc.)

PROFESSOR: You've been here six fuckin' months?

BABY SAN: Hey, man, I'm a computer operator.

PROFESSOR: Oh fuck, the guy's been skatin' for six months.

BABY SAN: Until a week ago I was living in an air-conditioned quonset hut in Saigon, man.

DINKY DAU: Air conditioning!

HABU: Williams, you motherfucker!!

BABY SAN: I pissed off my First Sergeant, so now I'm a grunt. Look, I don't wanna be here any more than you guys do, I was very happy in Saigon.

DINKY DAU: Well, no shit!

LITTLE JOHN: Baby San, you know where to find "autogetem" on your M–16?

(BABY SAN *looks at his M–16, points it at the* PROFESSOR. *The* PROFESSOR *hits the ground.* LITTLE JOHN *pushes the weapon away*)

PROFESSOR: That is not the way to find it.

LITTLE JOHN *(In a fatherly way)*: It's just two clicks from safe, Baby San. That's all I want to be thinkin' about while we're out there.

HABU: And if you have a great deal of trouble with that, just grab ahold of your ass and stick it in the ground!

BABY SAN: Stick my ass in the ground?

PROFESSOR: Try burying your shirt without taking it off. The effect is not at all dissimilar.

HABU: Little John, you better check that one's magazines.

LITTLE JOHN: Hell, I don't think he's even taped his dog tags, Habu. *(He gestures toward* BABY SAN's *magazine)* Are the first two rounds in your magazine tracers?

34

BABY SAN *(Blankly)*: Tracers?

HABU: Tracers. That's a bullet with an orange tip. When you fire it, it makes a red streak in the sky. You make the first two or three rounds tracers, that way when you see two red streaks in a row, you *know* you're runnin' outta ammo, it's time to reload. Little John, make sure he loads 'em all up proper *before* we go out. *(Pause)* Now, you two newbys stand up and hippity-hop up and down.

(DINKY DAU and BABY SAN get to their feet center stage and begin hopping in place. Clanking, clattering noises emanate from BABY SAN's equipment)

HABU: You gotta be bullshittin' me.

PROFESSOR: Baby San sounds like the Baja Marimba Band.

LITTLE JOHN: Like two skeletons fuckin' on a footlocker.

HABU: If I didn't know any better, I'd swear I hear a mess kit.

BABY SAN: I've got my mess kit, Tabu.

HABU: Dong lai . . . just fuckin' stop!

(They stop hopping. LITTLE JOHN fishes into BABY SAN's pack. He pulls out a steel mess kit)

LITTLE JOHN: Here it fuckin' is. *(He holds it up)* Wait, he's got boo-coo shit in here, Habu. *(He pulls out the items as he names them)* A camera—with flashcubes.

PROFESSOR: Oh, for night photography?

LITTLE JOHN: A transistor radio.

PROFESSOR: For the latest in sound!

LITTLE JOHN (*Pulls out maracas*): The Baja Marimba Band. *Wicked Sex (A magazine)* and a rubber ducky.

HABU: Lose the portable PX and the brain bucket. Scooter, check the other one.

(SCOOTER *begins checking out* DINKY DAU's *gear. All move in preparation to go on patrol and rattle off the following—addressing the two FNGs*)

PROFESSOR, LITTLE JOHN, SCOOTER, HABU (*Alternate lines*): All right, guys, tape down those sling swivels . . . Empty that change outta your pocket . . . Keep your ammo clean. Tracers—the ones with the orange tips. How you gonna know when you're outta ammo? Better smoke 'em while you got 'em. Pack that stuff quiet. Don't even dream about sleepin'. Tape those magazines butt to butt. Top off your canteens. I don't wanna hear no water sloshin'. Blouse your trouser bottoms. Be watchin' for trip wires. Eight fragmentation grenades. Twelve magazines. Two hundred rounds of ammo. Two clicks to "autogetem." If anything moves, you do it. Don't do anything stupid. Just follow your team leader. Keep your asses down! . . . Your team leader'll know what's happening . . . And whatever you do, don't be a hero.

(*Begin "Sympathy for the Devil" by the Rolling Stones. Music up*)

36

HABU: Scooter, my man, you got the point.

SCOOTER: Yeah, fuck it, man.

HABU: All right, get with your team leader. Team leader'll keep you alive, you keep him alive. We all come home alive. Load and lock. Let's get outta here and do this thing. *(All begin moving into patrol formation in slow motion)* And keep 'em at a decent interval this time. Let's move it out.

(All start to move about the stage in slow catlike fashion. Weapons poised, passing by, occasionally pointing at the audience. DINKY DAU *soliloquizes. The others pay no attention, concentrating on the business at hand. "Sympathy for the Devil" builds with his speech)*

DINKY DAU: I remember the sky was overcast. It was hot and muggy. Everyone's fatigues were drenched with sweat. It was late afternoon and we hadn't seen shit all day. I don't know what the hell I was thinking about right then, I guess my mind was just sorta blank at that point. I was so damn worn out—we all were. We'd been humpin' all day. My whole body was achin', I could hardly concentrate on the trail in front of me. The jungle on both sides of us started to get real dense, and the trail started goin' down-hill. Then all of a sudden, out of nowhere, there were twelve or maybe thirteen VC, right in front of us. *(*SCOOTER *suddenly freezes, points ahead. The others crouch down)* If the point man hadn't spotted them, they'd have walked right into us. I watched the point man as he raised his weapon. It was like a movie in slow motion. The point man opened up on the first two or three VC. *(*SCOOTER *opens fire. Music up with gunfire sound effects. The others open fire. All motions* *are slow and dreamlike)* I watched the first two or three VC go down, and then I opened up on full automatic. I creamed one of 'em with an entire clip. I watched my bullets as they ripped across his torso. Everybody was up. Everybody was hyper. Everybody was hittin'. *(He fumbles with his magazine)* Damn, I wasn't used to reloading. I couldn't get my clip in. Finally I got it.

SCOOTER *(Pointing)*: Hey, there's a couple of 'em gettin' away!

LITTLE JOHN: I got 'em.

DINKY DAU: Everyone was into it. I was eager. I was angry!

HABU: Security!

(The others cease firing. DINKY DAU presses forward)

DINKY DAU: It was the first time I killed anybody. There were eight or nine dead bodies lying on the ground, and I just kept blasting away at 'em. I just kept blasting away at 'em.

(HABU and the PROFESSOR grab him from behind. Music stops suddenly)

PROFESSOR: Save some ammo, man.

HABU: They ain't even gonna get any deader. *(To the others)* Spread out. Get a body count.

(DINKY DAU *stares at the bodies. The others begin sweeping the area*)

SCOOTER: I got three of 'em down here.

DINKY DAU: It was our little victory. Everybody really got off on that fact. Even the new guy, Baby San, who had a bad case of the combat shakes.

(BABY SAN *to* LITTLE JOHN, *his hands shaking*)

BABY SAN: Hey, Little John, my hands are shakin' like crazy. But I don't feel scared. I don't feel fuckin' nothin'.

LITTLE JOHN: Don't worry about it, Baby San. It'll be like that till you get used to it.

PROFESSOR: Two in the bushes.

(*All begin checking out the bodies.* DINKY DAU *in center, the others encircling him*)

DINKY DAU: It was our little victory!

PROFESSOR: It was our little victory!

DINKY DAU: Eight or nine of the little motherfuckers and not one of us even got a scratch.

LITTLE JOHN: . . . not a scratch.

DINKY DAU: You're dead, motherfucker!

LITTLE JOHN: You're dead, motherfucker!

DINKY DAU: Don't fuck with me!

SCOOTER: Don't fuck with me!

DINKY DAU: Teach those little motherfuckers!

DINKY DAU and HABU *(Simultaneously)*: Think you can walk down my trail in the middle of the day? Who the fuck do you think you are?!

DINKY DAU: Guys were rippin' up their gear. Breakin' weapons.

HABU: Breakin' weapons.

DINKY DAU: Dumping rice all over the ground.

SCOOTER: Dumping rice.

DINKY DAU: Kickin' bodies.

PROFESSOR: Kickin' bodies.

DINKY DAU: Hey, gotta make sure they're dead, right? They were keeping little souvenirs.

BABY SAN: Hey, Little John, look at this fuckin' belt buckle. *(Pause)* Hey, what are you doin', Scooter, cuttin' his ears off?

SCOOTER: Yeah, you want one, Baby San?

BABY SAN: No . . .

(DINKY DAU *stares at the bodies. Fade: "Sympathy for the Devil" back in)*

DINKY DAU: Eight or nine dead VC. They were so shot up I couldn't even recognize the one I remember hitting.

HABU: Let's saddle up. Let's get outta here.

(*All start to exit slowly.* HABU's *radio call fades as he exits)*

HABU: Okay, let's move it out. Stockdale, Stockdale, this is India Two Bravo. Over *(Pause)* We have zero niner enemy confirms and zero two probables. Over.

(DINKY DAU *now alone onstage. Lights begin to fade)*

DINKY DAU: It's okay. It's okay, Alex. I know he would've killed me if he had the chance. Dear God, I know that little gook motherfucker would've killed me if he had the chance . . . (*He is overcome with emotion. As lights fade, he repeats line)* He would've killed me if he had the chance. I know he would've.

(*Music up and out. Fade to black or cross-fade)*

The Fourth of July

Shadowy lighting up. DINKY DAU, SCOOTER, *and* LITTLE JOHN *are asleep in the hootch.* DINKY DAU *wakes with a start, as if from a nightmare.*

DINKY DAU: Mama! Mama!! *(He gets up, mutters to himself, and starts rummaging through an ammo can full of C rations)* Ah! Beans and dicks. Chocolate-fuckin'-nut roll. Peanut butter. How's a guy supposed to eat this shit?! Holy shit, a fuckin' pound cake! *(He crosses to* SCOOTER, *who is still asleep. In an excited whisper)* Hey, Scooter! I got a pound cake here, and I'll tell you what I'm gonna do. I'm gonna split this pound with you, if you split a can of peaches with me.

SCOOTER *(Sleepily)*: What? What time is it?

DINKY DAU: Look, fuck what time it is, man! I'm talkin' peaches and pound cake, motherfucker.

SCOOTER: Aren't they servin' chow pretty soon?

DINKY DAU: Fuck that shit chow! Who can eat that shit, anyway? I'm talkin' peaches and fuckin' pound cake, motherfucker.

SCOOTER: I haven't got anything left except some ham and motherfuckers, man. You can have that shit. Gimme some slack.

DINKY DAU: I got a great idea. Why don't you get up off your lazy ass and check it out, man.

SCOOTER: Dinky Dau, I ate all my fruit on the last patrol. Lemme get some z's, man.

DINKY DAU: That's it! I know what we can do. We'll go down to the LZ, man, and rip off a case of C rats. Okay, let's see. You can have all the spaghetti and meatballs, and the beans 'n dicks, and I get all the fruit.

SCOOTER: Slack!

DINKY DAU: Okay, okay, dildo-brain, you can have some fuckin' fruit, man . . . but you gotta choose between pears and apricots, 'cause I've got dibs on the motherfuckin' peaches.

SCOOTER: Slack!

DINKY DAU: Scooter, I am here to tell you, you are one big broken-dick motherfucker, man. *(He stops and approaches* LITTLE JOHN. *Whispers)* Say, Little John . . . peaches and pound cake, motherfucker. Doesn't that sound great, man?

LITTLE JOHN: Do I look like I want any fuckin' peaches and pound cake, Dinky Dau? *(He and* SCOOTER *go back to sleep)*

DINKY DAU: I'm livin' with two big broken-dick motherfuckers. Just wait until another offer like this comes along. And keep your fuckin' paws off my pound cake. *(He crosses to his sleeping area, sits. Music begins: "Sympathy for the Devil." He addresses audience)* I couldn't get to sleep that night. I just wanted to talk to someone about what happened. You see, I kept flashing back on those bodies, and that one guy. I can still see the bullets ripping across his torso. Like I had a license to kill, huh? But he was a human being. I'm a human being?! I really lost it there for a minute. I was shooting at dead bodies. I was shooting at men I knew were already dead. It's a terrible sight to see a man's body get ripped apart like that. It was a frenzy that I got caught up in. *(Music up)* A crazy, primal, stupid, fuckin' frenzy. A frenzy of killing!

(Music up full. Lights cross-fade. BABY SAN *enters excitedly. He is wearing a Vietnamese hat. In the shadowy light, he could be mistaken for a Vietnamese)*

BABY SAN *(Tapping* DINKY DAU *on the shoulder from behind)*: Hey, Dinky Dau.

*(*DINKY DAU *turns and attacks him)*

BABY SAN *(Taking the hat off)*: Hello!

DINKY DAU: Where'd you get this fuckin' hat, man?

BABY SAN: Saigon, man.

DINKY DAU: Hm, not bad.

BABY SAN: Yeah, Saigon not bad, either. What's goin' on with these broken-dicks?

DINKY DAU: Fuckin' broken-dicks is right, man. I offered 'em peaches and pound cake and look at 'em.

BABY SAN: Watch this.

DINKY DAU: What're you gonna do?

BABY SAN *(Banging on an ammo can. Loudly)*: Wake up broken-dicks!

(SCOOTER *and* LITTLE JOHN *wake up with a start, grabbing for their weapons*)

DINKY DAU: Don't shoot, it's us!

(They relax)

BABY SAN: I brought back a special fuckin' treat, guys!

DINKY DAU: What is it?

BABY SAN: Real fuckin' charcoal incense.

LITTLE JOHN: That's our big treat, Baby San?

BABY SAN: This is the real stuff, man. This is the stuff the Vietnamese Buddhists use in their religious ceremonies.

SCOOTER: Yeah. Well, who gives a shit?

DINKY DAU: Where'd you get it?

BABY SAN: A little apothecary shop in Saigon. The papasan could barely speak English. The only way I could get him to understand "incense" was by stickin' my fingers up my nose and sniffin'.

LITTLE JOHN *(Takes a sniff of the white powder)*: It doesn't smell like anything, Baby San.

BABY SAN: You gotta put it over burning charcoal first.

(DINKY DAU *takes a pinch of the powder and carefully tastes it*)

SCOOTER: You mean we gotta find some charcoal?

BABY SAN: Fuck you guys, it's a present.

DINKY DAU: Check this out, Scooter.

SCOOTER: This ain't incense, Baby San, it's fuckin' skag!!

BABY SAN: What?

DINKY DAU: This is heroin, Baby San. Incense. I can't believe you, man!

SCOOTER (*Takes a taste*): It's numbah-one shit, Baby San.

DINKY DAU: How much did you pay for this "incense," Baby San?

BABY SAN: Two cartons of Salems.

SCOOTER: There's enough shit here to fuck up the entire squad for at least a week.

BABY SAN: Stupid fuckin' papasan. I thought he knew exactly what I wanted.

DINKY DAU: You're not planning on taking this shit back, are you?

BABY SAN: Where? I couldn't even find that little place again.

DINKY DAU: Tell you what, Baby San. Look under my rack, there's a few cartons of Salems there. I've been savin' 'em for something just like this.

BABY SAN: You keep 'em. It's yours.

LITTLE JOHN: Wait a second . . . you guys ain't planning on (DINKY DAU *snorts some up*) taking that stuff?

DINKY DAU: Little John, we're just gonna get down a little bit. No big fuckin' deal. *(He takes another snort)*

LITTLE JOHN: But you don't even know what's in it.

DINKY DAU: So?

LITTLE JOHN *(Alarmed, looking at* DINKY DAU's *face)*: Hey, what's happenin' to your face? Hey, Baby San, come here, look at this.

BABY SAN: What?

DINKY DAU *(Alarmed)*: What?! What is it, man?! What's wrong with my face?!

LITTLE JOHN: You've got fuckin' hair growin' out of it.

*(*SCOOTER *and* BABY SAN *roll with laughter)*

DINKY DAU *(To* LITTLE JOHN*)*: You asshole! You scared the shit out of me, dildo-brain!

47

LITTLE JOHN: You guys ain't even worried about getting addicted?

DINKY DAU: Little John, what did I just get through tellin' you? We're just gonna get down a little bit. No big deal, man. *(Pause)* Hey, why don't you try some, I bet you'd get into it.

LITTLE JOHN: Fuck no, I don't need that shit! *(He grabs for and opens a whiskey bottle and slugs)*

DINKY DAU: Baby San, how 'bout you? You wanna try some?

BABY SAN: I'll give it a try. Whatta you gotta do, just snort it up?

DINKY DAU: That's right, you just snort it up.

SCOOTER: It just mellows you out a little bit, Baby San.

*(*BABY SAN *snorts long and hard)*

LITTLE JOHN: What do you think that shit would cost back in the world?

DINKY DAU: Boo-coo bucks, man.

SCOOTER: Maybe five, six hundred dollars.

LITTLE JOHN: So what happens if you get hooked and you're back in the world? Where you gonna find five hundred dollars every time you want to get high?

SCOOTER: You don't get hooked, just doin' it a few times.

LITTLE JOHN: You don't know what could happen after one time. You don't even know what the fuck it is! You guys are stupid!

DINKY DAU: Go drink your booze, man. *(To* BABY SAN*)* Can you feel it, Baby San?

LITTLE JOHN *(Mocking* DINKY DAU*)*: Can you feel it, Baby San?

DINKY DAU: Fuck you, man! Baby San, like in the back of your throat, just sorta dripping down?

BABY SAN: I think I better do just a little bit more. *(He takes another long snort. He gets to his feet and starts to space out with broad physical movements)*

DINKY DAU: You gettin' off, Baby San?

BABY SAN: I'm feelin' a little bit weird, Dinky Dau.

LITTLE JOHN: Gettin' off? Shit, you guys really look like you're gettin' off.

DINKY DAU: Would you get off it, man?! It's like the way we feel deep down inside, man. Something a juicer wouldn't know nothing the fuck about!

BABY SAN *(Starts to sing)*: "Ma-ri-a! I just met a girl named Maria!"

DINKY DAU: That's what I'm talkin' about, man! *(He joins* BABY SAN *in the worst, most outrageous rendition of "Maria" ever sung. Three verses and then he cuts it off. Softly)* "Maria . . . I'll never stop saying Maria . . ."

BABY SAN *(Softly)*: Tony, Tony, Tony!

DINKY DAU *(Shoves* BABY SAN *away)*: Get outta here, man. We gotta get serious with this shit. Baby San, do you really wanna experience this high?

*(*BABY SAN *continues to space out and improvise)*

DINKY DAU: I'm talkin' to you, man.

BABY SAN: Yeah, I'll give it a try.

DINKY DAU: Hey, Scooter, how about you?

SCOOTER: Yeah, fuck it. *(He produces a spoon and syringe and hands them to* DINKY DAU*)*

DINKY DAU: Snorting's too fuckin' half-assed, man. Baby San, come here. *(*BABY SAN *crosses to* DINKY DAU. SCOOTER *picks up a camera and starts taking pictures of them and the skag)* Hey, Scooter, don't be takin' no pictures over here, man. We'll all end up in LBJ. Now, Baby San, watch what I'm doin'. You gotta liquefy it first.

BABY SAN: Whatta you gonna do? Shoot it up, Dinky Dau?

DINKY DAU: Yeah, that's right, I'm gonna shoot it up. And if you're diggin' on it now, you should see what it feels like when you shoot up, man. It's like the same high, except a lot more intense, 'cause you get it all in a rush at one time. *(He pours the liquefied substance into the syringe)* Okay now, this is where I need your help. Take off your belt. (BABY SAN *is spacing out on his belt)* Hurry up, man, this shit doesn't last all night once you heat it up. (BABY SAN *continues to space out)* Will you stop fuckin' around! Now tie it around my arm, just tight enough to catch a vein. Okay now, you see right here . . . that's where you're gonna put it in. *(He offers the syringe to BABY SAN)*

BABY SAN: Me? I don't think I can shoot anybody up, Dinky Dau.

DINKY DAU: Some friend. Fuck it. I'll do it myself, no big fuckin' deal, man.

(He lowers the needle toward his arm. LITTLE JOHN grabs his hand, attempting to stop him from shooting up)

LITTLE JOHN: Do you know what the fuck you're doing?

DINKY DAU: Look, if you don't like it, Little John, just dee-dee fuckin' mau outta here.

BABY SAN: Dee-dee mau, Little John.

DINKY DAU: Why don't you go and get shit-faced with the rest of your juicer friends, if this is against your principles.

LITTLE JOHN: Fuck principles! I'm just tryin' to tell you that you're gonna fuck up your vein if you stick it in like that.

DINKY DAU: And how the fuck would you know? . . . Wait a minute, I almost forgot. This here is Mr. Two Years of Pre-Med School.

BABY SAN: Oh, pre-med!

DINKY DAU: Mr. Expert on the Subject.

BABY SAN: We have an expert among us!

DINKY DAU: Well, since you know so much the fuck about it, would you do it for me? C'mon, you're the expert! *(Pause)* Please. I'm gonna fuck up my vein if I stick it in there like that.

(LITTLE JOHN *takes the syringe. He pours whiskey on* DINKY DAU*'s arm to sterilize it*)

LITTLE JOHN: Dinky Dau, if you wanna be a junkie, that's your fuckin' business. *(He readies the needle)* You sure you want this?

DINKY DAU: Just do it, man.

BABY SAN: Just do it, man.

LITTLE JOHN: Okay.

DINKY DAU: C'mon, man, just do it!

(LITTLE JOHN *injects the fluid.* DINKY DAU *keels over.* BABY SAN *catches him*)

BABY SAN: It's that fast! (DINKY DAU *vomits in* BABY SAN's *lap*. BABY SAN *jumps*) Oh, my God, he's throwing up on me.

LITTLE JOHN: Looks like a lot of fun, doesn't it, Baby San?

SCOOTER: Hey, man, fuckin' peaches!

DINKY DAU (*Slowly gets up with* BABY SAN's *help*): Oh, man. Baby San, like I'm flying . . . like right after I did it . . .

LITTLE JOHN: Right after you did it, you puked all over your goddamn self.

BABY SAN: He did not, he puked all over *me*.

DINKY DAU: Baby San, it's like being in a cartoon. It's like havin' sex in slow motion.

BABY SAN: Get off of me, then!

DINKY DAU: The rush, man. You can't believe the rush, man. What a rush!

BABY SAN: Dinky Dau, I think I'm just gonna snort up a little more, okay?

DINKY DAU: Let's go down to the river and go swimmin'. I wanna go swimmin', man! It's better than killin' people. Let's go swimmin'! I just wanna go swimmin'.

BABY SAN: Swimmin'? He wants to go swimmin'! We can't go swimmin', man! It's nighttime. There's a lot of little bad guys runnin' around out there. I got an idea. Let's go out on the bunker and look at the tracers. You wanna do that?

DINKY DAU: That's a beautiful idea, man! (BABY SAN *attempts to help him to his feet*) This is great, man. Oh, what a rush, man!

BABY SAN: You guys wanna come with us?

DINKY DAU: What a rush!

BABY SAN: Hurry up, he's in a rush!

(*All join together arm in arm for walk "outside." Sound and lights change to simulate tracers and flares around the perimeter*)

DINKY DAU: It's the fuckin' Fourth of July, motherfuckers.

BABY SAN: Every day here is the Fourth of July.

DINKY DAU (*Starts singing*): "I'm a Yankee Doodle Dandy . . ."

(*All join in*)

ALL: "A Yankee Doodle, do or die
A real live nephew of my Uncle Sam,
Born on the Fourth of July . . ."

(DINKY DAU *vomits again. Music in: "The Star Spangled Banner" by Jimi Hendrix. All stand and look at the tracers. Slowly they turn toward the gun rack . . .*)

Touchdown

Lights cross-fade. HABU *and* PROFESSOR *enter. They get into patrol formation with weapons poised. Spotlight on* HABU. *Faint music.*

HABU *(To audience)*: They call 'em patrols, I call them hunting parties. That's what we do, you know . . . hunt 'em, kill 'em, and count 'em. If we lose any, we count them, too. Then we call in the count and we get points. Where does it all go? I think it goes to a big computerized scoreboard, and every day the big brass go in and they look at it. They nod their big heads and they say, "Ah, very good hunting, boys." How do I feel? It's my team against his. And a kill is just a touchdown, man. *Fuck it.*

(Gunfire, lights, and smoke effects. Actors move about responding to an attack. Lights fade to black. Music up: "Magic Carpet Ride" by Steppenwolf)

ACT TWO

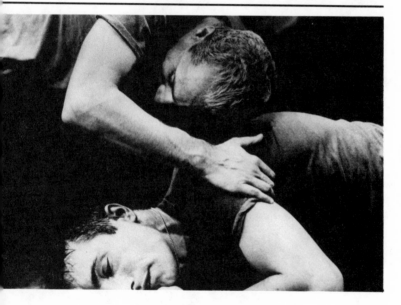

Music ("Light My Fire" by the Doors) fades. DINKY DAU *and* BABY SAN *sit on the floor playing a game of gin.*

DINKY DAU: I'm so fuckin' bored I could scream.

BABY SAN: Scream, Dinky Dau?

(Both scream at the top of their voices. The feeling is relief)

DINKY DAU: Ah. *(Pause)* My girlfriend is drivin' me crazy. A couple of weeks ago I get a letter from her—she tells me she wants to be a teacher. Then last week she tells me she wants to be a waitress. Is that con-fuckin'-fused or what?! *(He deals the cards)*

BABY SAN: Dinky Dau, I think I got the hootch maid pregnant.

DINKY DAU: Ah, Baby San, if I don't get outta here soon, I'm gonna beg 'em to send me back out into the fuckin' bush.

BABY SAN: She told me this morning, right in the middle of . . . you know.

DINKY DAU: And that fuckin' mystery meat they served for chow last night. How's a guy supposed to eat that shit? All I want is a nice, thick, juicy steak; maybe some french fries on the side.

BABY SAN: I suppose what I should do is take her to the Med Battalion. Maybe Doc Case will take a look at her. I'll give him a bag of pot.

DINKY DAU: And what I wouldn't do for some real eggs. You remember, the ones with the shells on 'em? And some real ham. And if I could sit down one morning and eat my breakfast without sixty guys hangin' all over me. Hey, pass the salt and pepper! Hey, fuck you, asshole!

BABY SAN: I'm sure I could get her over to the Med Battalion. Shit, what if she is? I mean, you know, I don't love her. We only done it one time. Maybe I'm a little bit horny. What'll I tell Julie?

DINKY DAU: Did I tell you I'm on fuckin' shit-burning detail all this week? Stick it up your ass, Williams, you lifer-cocksucker!

BABY SAN: This could fuck up my entire life. 'Cause now she's saying, "Oh, Baby San, you takey me to America." Yeah, my pop's gonna love that shit. You know what he's gonna say? . . . He's gonna say, "Hey, Kris, she don't *look* Italian."

DINKY DAU: And that fuckin' Williams—pulled my pass to Saigon. What do they think I am, a fuckin' hermit?! I was gonna get my first piece of ass . . . *(Pause)* in this country. You're a son-of-a-bitch, Williams, and you fuckin' know it, you fat little fucker!

BABY SAN: Now she's sayin' we could send for her folks. We got papasan, mamasan, soon we'll have a little babysan. I don't think I love her . . . and we only done it twice.

DINKY DAU: Workin' in that fuckin' Orderly Room seven days a week. Day in, day out. How much can a guy take? I need a fuckin' rest!

BABY SAN: Hey, you don't think she's trying to use me as a ticket to the States? I mean, okay, we done it five times . . . and I know I don't love her.

DINKY DAU: I know what I'll do. I'll find his fuckin' 201 file . . . I'll tear his finance records into little bitty pieces and burn them in that shitter this afternoon. Ha! You can't leave the country without your records, Williams! *Life in Vietnam!!*

(The following two lines overlap)

BABY SAN: I think you're right, Dinky Dau! Sure, naïve Baby San, think I'm some kind of sucker? That little gook!

DINKY DAU: That's right! I'll show them! I'll show that fuckin' Williams. *Nobody* fucks with Dinky Dau! You got that? Don't fuck with me!

61

(The lines build to BABY SAN *throwing his cards down)*

BABY SAN: Gin! *(He starts to exit)*

DINKY DAU *(Angry and loud)*: C'mon, deal another hand. I never beat you.

BABY SAN *(Angry)*: I just got done tellin' you, I got some business to attend to.

DINKY DAU: Yeah, I got some business, too.

BABY SAN: Yeah, I'll catch you Tuesday. I gotta drive some colonel to fuckin' Saigon.

DINKY DAU: Yeah. Well, have a nice trip.

BABY SAN: Maybe I will. *(Exits)*

DINKY DAU *(Picking up the cards, muttering to himself)*: I never fuckin' beat him. He must be cheatin' . . . *Saigon!? Saigon!?* How the fuck did you get to go to Saigon?! Asshole! Get back here . . . ! *(He exits angrily)*

(Music up: "Light My Fire." Blackout)

In the Rear with the Beer and the Gear

Low Music. Cross-fade: LITTLE JOHN *addresses audience. Spotlight on him.*

LITTLE JOHN: Well. Been out in the fuckin' bush for ten fuckin' days. Fuckin' choppers picked us up outta a fuckin' rice paddy, flew us back to fuckin' Charlie III fuckin' combat base. Fuckin' six said we done fuckin' good. Fuckin' number one. Gonna get us some Cinder-fuckin'-ella-fuckin' liberty. So we went and got us a fuckin' shower and some clean fuckin' fatigues, and hitched us a fuckin' ride into the fuckin' ville. Found us a fuckin' bar and hoisted ourselves a fuckin' few. After careful fuckin' consideration, we decided what we really wanted to fuckin' do was get fuckin' laid. So we went and found us a fuckin' massage parlor; talked to the fuckin' mamasan; gave her some fuckin' P; she brought out her fuckin' girls. Fuckin' number-one sik lou girls. I picked out a fuckin' girl, we went behind the fuckin' curtains, took off our fuckin' clean fuckin' fatigues, laid down on the fuckin' mats—and we made love.

(Music up: "Light My Fire." Blackout)

Cheryl's Letter

Lights up: low music. In the hootch. DINKY DAU *enters excitedly with a letter in his hand. He opens it and reads aloud to himself.*

DINKY DAU: "Dear Alex, Hi." *(He says "Hi" back to her aloud)* "I got your letter a couple of days ago. I'm sorry that it rains on you so much. I can't imagine not having a dry pair of socks to put on. I'm sorry it's been so long since I've written, but a lot of things have been happening. They raised the tuition here, and I don't think I can afford it. I guess I'll have to start looking for another school. I still haven't decided what I want to major in. I thought about sociology, but one of my professors said he didn't think I'd make a good social worker, because he thought I would sympathize with the people too much. *(He chuckles and says yeah to himself)* Oh well. I went to a mixer about a month ago at State. Remember Roger? The guy on the basketball team in my high school that we used to call the Flash? Well, he's playing soccer now, and the whole team was at the mixer. Alex, I have to tell you that I've been dating Roger. [*Pause*] We double with Lisa and Jim, or we do things in a group with the soccer team, like go to a party or something. I feel bad, Alex, because you're so far away. And real guilty, too. I'll still write to you so that you'll have someone write to. I'm really sorry. I just had to tell you. I hope we can still be friends and that you'll come to see me when you get back. Well, I have to close now, because I have to write a term paper for English Comp, yuk. I'm really sorry. Love, Cheryl." *(He repeats the following words a few times)* "Alex, I have to tell you that I've been dating Roger!" What did I do? What did I do, man? "Alex, I have to tell you that I've been dating Roger."

(SCOOTER *and* BABY SAN *enter excitedly.* DINKY DAU *stuffs the letter into his pocket and hides his feelings)*

BABY SAN: Hey, Dinky Dau, I got the jeep.

SCOOTER: Steam 'n cream, partner.

DINKY DAU: Are you guys goin' down to the massage parlor?

BABY SAN: Fuckin' A, man. I got my cum catcher *(Shows a prophylactic and exits)*

SCOOTER *(Takes* DINKY DAU's *arm)*: C'mon, man, steam 'n cream. *(He sees the letter. They have a moment of understanding)*

DINKY DAU: I guess I'll be meeting you guys down there this time, Scooter. *(*SCOOTER *exits. Crumbles up letter and tosses it)* Fuck you. *(Exits)*

(Music up: "Light My Fire." Cross-fade)

Friends

Lights up: The PROFESSOR *sits alone, reading* Steppenwolf. *Music up: "Four and Twenty" by Crosby, Stills, Nash & Young.* BABY SAN *enters. He's shuffling a deck of cards and singing loudly and very badly. Music fades out.*

BABY SAN *(Singing)*: "When you're a jet, you're a jet all the way." *(Stops singing)* Hey, Professor. How ya doing? Seen Dinky Dau around?

PROFESSOR *(Answers without looking up)*: Nope.

BABY SAN: How 'bout Little John?

PROFESSOR: I believe he went down to the EM Club.

BABY SAN: Oh. How 'bout Scooter?

PROFESSOR: Scooter went with him.

BABY SAN: Wanna go down and join 'em? C'mon, let's go. Get ourselves a beer!

PROFESSOR: No thanks, Baby San.

BABY SAN: Wanna play some gin?

PROFESSOR *(Losing patience)*: No, Baby San.

BABY SAN: Whatcha reading? Something by that Italian guy, Panangangenellio?

PROFESSOR: Actually, he preferred to be called Pirandello.

BABY SAN: Oh. *(He looks over his shoulder and spots the title of the book)* Steppenwolf! I didn't know they wrote a book about these guys already! *(He grabs the book)* Any pictures?

PROFESSOR: This one has nothing to do with the rock 'n' roll band, Baby San.

(The PROFESSOR *takes back the book.* BABY SAN *looks over his shoulder again)*

BABY SAN *(Reading)*: Hermann Hess-y.

PROFESSOR: *Hess-e.* It's pronounced, Hermann *Hess-e.*

BABY SAN: Hermann Hess-e, uh. He write some pretty good shit, this guy?

PROFESSOR: Yes, Baby San. As you have so eloquently phrased it, he wrote some wonderfully "good shit." I'm reading it for the third time.

BABY SAN (*Laughs*): You're shittin' me! You read this whole fuckin' book *three* times!? Three times, one book three times! (*Pause*) I've seen *West Side Story* eight times, but that's a movie.

PROFESSOR: Anyone ever tell you you could be a cretin?

BABY SAN: No. Sometimes I get taken for Jewish, though.

PROFESSOR: What?

BABY SAN: Let's play some gin. C'mon, man, one quick game.

PROFESSOR: Baby San, I do not want to play gin!

BABY SAN (*Begins dealing the cards*): C'mon, man, just one game.

PROFESSOR: No.

BABY SAN: Why not? Don't you know how to play, Professor?

PROFESSOR: Yes, I know how to play, but I'm preoccupied with something else at the moment.

BABY SAN: Just one game.

67

PROFESSOR: What does it take to get through to you, man? This is the English language—emphatically—*no gin. No fuckin' gin!*

BABY SAN: Do you have some kind of problem, Professor?

PROFESSOR: Yes, I have a problem—I'm trying to concentrate on a fuckin' book, and a pest named Baby San keeps throwing cards at me.

BABY SAN: No, man, that's not what I mean. Do you have a problem? How many really close friends would you say you have in 'Nam?

PROFESSOR *(Resentful)*: What is this?

BABY SAN: I'm just trying to help you. Like whenever we're not on patrol, I always see you sittin' around here by your lonesome. You're not tight with anybody.

PROFESSOR: I can do without your help. Don't fuck with me, Baby San.

BABY SAN *(Gathers up his cards, stands, and starts to exit)*: I'm gonna go down to the EM Club and have a beer. You have a wonderful afternoon. You and all your little friends, Parananaganellio, Hermann Hess-y, and *Steppenwolf*, the book. *(Exits. Lights fade. Music up)*

PROFESSOR: Baby San, I have been able to make some friends here. I just don't like to get too close to people.

(Music louder: "Light My Fire." Fade lights to black. A loud explosion is heard in the blackout)

Blanket Party

Music: "Light My Fire." Lights up on a tableau of BABY SAN, LITTLE JOHN, DINKY DAU, *and the* PROFESSOR. *Lighting should be surreal until action begins. Sergeant* WILLIAMS *is spotlit separately and away from the group. Each character is frozen in a position that is the physical manifestation of each actor/veteran's response to seeing dead bodies all over the stage. No bodies or props should be used. Spot on* WILLIAMS.

WILLIAMS: Eighty percent are targets.

(Spot out. WILLIAMS *exits)*

BABY SAN *(Begins to move across the stage, stepping over bodies)*: Worse than shit! (LITTLE JOHN *alters physical position and freezes)* Like rotting onions. *(The* PROFESSOR *alters physical position and freezes)* Sweet, burning meat . . . (DINKY DAU *alters physical position and freezes)* I once looked at the floor of a butcher's shop.

LITTLE JOHN: Let's just get this over with. *(They pair off:* LITTLE JOHN *and* DINKY DAU, BABY SAN *and the* PROFESSOR) We'll put the whole ones in a pile over there. *(Pause)* Dinky Dau.

PROFESSOR: C'mon, Baby San.

(They pantomime picking up bodies and stacking them in the area that LITTLE JOHN *indicated. For a few beats the task is carried out in silence. The following dialogue occurs while they are moving and stacking bodies)*

BABY SAN: Hey, Professor.

PROFESSOR: Yeah?

BABY SAN: My R&R came through.

PROFESSOR: Yeah, where are you going?

BABY SAN: Hong Kong.

PROFESSOR: That's great. When are you leaving?

BABY SAN: Two weeks. In two weeks I'm gonna be in fuckin' Hong Kong. *(He drops his end of the body and turns away abruptly)*

PROFESSOR: C'mon. You okay?

BABY SAN *(To himself)*: That guy . . . he looked just like me. I can't believe I'm talkin' about goin' on my R&R.

LITTLE JOHN *(Spreading out a blanket on the ground)*: Let's get the rest of it. Everybody grab a corner of the blanket. Baby San, you too.

BABY SAN: Little John, I think I'm gonna be sick.

LITTLE JOHN: Nobody likes to be on a blanket-party detail, Baby San, but somebody's gotta do it. If you're gonna get sick, just go over to those bushes—we'll wait up for you.

BABY SAN: I . . . I'll let you know.

(All bend down; begin picking up dismembered parts, tossing them on the blanket)

BABY SAN *(Picks up a piece of flesh and soliloquizes)*: Like . . . red Jell-O . . . wet. Sticky. Gray. Slimy. Dripping out. Oozing out.

DINKY DAU: I feel like a garbage collector.

BABY SAN: All brown and watery . . . and I lost my sense of judgment yesterday.

PROFESSOR: Look at this . . . a finger, just . . . a finger.

DINKY DAU: Hey, Baby San.

BABY SAN *(With a start)*: What?

DINKY DAU: You shoulda picked Australia instead of Hong Kong.

BABY SAN: What?

DINKY DAU: What do you mean, "What"? Free pussy, man. And round-eyed women. Everybody speaks English. I was there in April. I had a boo-coo number-fuckin'-one, outta-sight time. If you go to Hong Kong, man, those assholes are just gonna rip you off. Go to Australia.

BABY SAN: Maybe next time.

LITTLE JOHN (*Picks up something, looks at it*): I wonder who this one belongs to? Let's hold it up—I'm gonna check this out.

(*He leans over a whole body, holding an arm in one hand; others look in his direction*)

PROFESSOR: Check it out?!

(BABY SAN, *off to one side of stage, becomes nauseated*)

DINKY DAU: Hey, Little John, what's the difference?

LITTLE JOHN: Whatta y'all think? This one here?

BABY SAN: Uh huh.

DINKY DAU: Little John, what's the fuckin' difference?

LITTLE JOHN: I've got two bodies here that don't have any arms. Doesn't it make sense that this belongs to *one* of them?

PROFESSOR: This is nuts!

LITTLE JOHN: Well, say one of those guys was you. Wouldn't you rather have your folks back home get something that looks like a whole body, instead of something that looks like a slab of meat?

(BABY SAN, *by this time, vomiting*)

DINKY DAU: You're the one that's crazy! You're the one who's fuckin' dinky dau.

LITTLE JOHN: I ain't gonna fuckin' argue about it. *(He turns his attention back to the bodies)* I'm almost sure it belongs to this one.

DINKY DAU: And what if it doesn't belong to that one? Then what are you gonna do?

LITTLE JOHN: Then what fuckin' difference does it make? You can't tell 'em apart, anyway!

PROFESSOR: I can't believe I'm hearing this. I can't even watch this.

DINKY DAU: That stupid asshole thinks he's playing with a jigsaw puzzle. *(To* LITTLE JOHN*)* That's a human being you're fuckin' around with!

LITTLE JOHN: I know it's a human being. That's why I'm doing it!

DINKY DAU: Hey, hey, Little John! While we're here . . . *(He takes a piece from the blanket)* . . . why don't you see if you can fit this in your fucking jigsaw puzzle. *(He throws the piece at* LITTLE JOHN*)*

LITTLE JOHN: You gone crazy?! You really are fuckin' *dinky dau*, aren't you?

DINKY DAU: Here's another nice chunk for you to fuck around with.

He tosses another piece. LITTLE JOHN *dodges. They shout threats at each other while* DINKY DAU *continues tossing pieces at* LITTLE JOHN. LITTLE JOHN *rushes* DINKY DAU. *They engage in a brief scuffle, culminating with both men falling on the blanket.* BABY SAN, *by this time, has stopped vomiting. The scuffle ceases.* DINKY DAU *and* LITTLE JOHN *look disgusted. They slowly get to their feet)*

PROFESSOR: Number-fuckin'-one! *(Pause)* Get this garbage off your shirt.

DINKY DAU: This is stupid, Little John! I'm sorry. This is fuckin' stupid! Please don't ask me to do this detail anymore.

PROFESSOR: Can we please just get this over with?!

(All four get around the blanket and reach for the corners. Music up: "Unknown Soldier" by the Doors. They lift the blanket slowly and carry it offstage ritualistically. All exit except the PROFESSOR*)*

(Lights cross-fade. Music cross-fades to Vietnamese music)

Parallel Vietnam Ambiguities

Lights spot the PROFESSOR. *He addresses the audience.*

PROFESSOR: The plastic explosive claymore mind conjures up another day of technological improbable war-in-the-mud. Is Napalm Nellie a new dance, or the name of Roy Rogers's jeep? A homeward-oriented vision of myriad anachronisms, brought to you by today's desperate fantasy ball. Proper attire being jungle camouflage. Bring your own weapon. The lethal extension of a mutated, omnipresent ego. Buddha is hiding in every round, Christ climbed off his pedestal, and God is a can of beer. That blinding flash of light and deafening crack means that razor-sharp chunks of metal are screaming in your direction, permeating the air with melodies of blood. The anonymous witch of your childhood nightmares piercing your heart with long, pointed fingernails, ripping the lips off your face. We live daily in our subterranean, rat-infested bunkers, trapped spirits on the periphery of obscurity, the true definition of surrealism. Time on a shivering-wet, isolated, starless, black-perimeter-guard-duty night is not a theoretical fourth dimension. It's a self-propelled hammer and anvil somewhere between the temples, an ephemeral black-smith pounding out another Kafkaesque minute after minute. I maintain a precarious balance on the very edge of sanity. And I see through the crack in the mirror; I see through to her, holding me and brushing my cheek with her fingertips and whispering an ever sweet and gentle lie: "I love you." *Halt!* Who goes there? I do. Apprehensively walking toward myself. Frightened by the prospect that I, we, might someday meet.

Professor and Doc

Lights up on hootch area. Music up: "Four and Twenty." DOC is sitting reading Steppenwolf. *He wears a battered fatigue shirt with peace symbols painted on it, beads, etc. . . . He is the classic hippie GI. The* PROFESSOR *enters the area apprehensively.* DOC *heaves a sigh. Music fades.*

DOC: He went down to the skivvy house.

PROFESSOR *(Seems bewildered)*: What?

DOC: I said he went down to the skivvy house. He said you should meet him down there, you can get the clap together.

PROFESSOR: I just came up here for my malaria pill.

DOC *(Plops down the book)*: Oh, sorry about that shit.

(He crosses to get the pill. The PROFESSOR *picks up the book)*

PROFESSOR *(To himself)*: Far fuckin' out.

(DOC crosses back to the PROFESSOR, *takes the book, and hands him the pill)*

DOC: Far fuckin' out. The Steppenwolf will not prevent malaria. *(He sits with the book)* Have a very pleasant afternoon and a wonderful shit. Later.

PROFESSOR *(Starts to exit. Re-enters)*: Sorry to bother you again. I hate to bring this up. *(He shows* DOC *his finger)* I woke up with it this morning.

DOC (*Examines it closely*): It's a rat bite.

PROFESSOR: But it's not a very deep one!

DOC: Deep enough, my man.

PROFESSOR: What happens now?

DOC: Anti-rabies treatment.

PROFESSOR: The shots I've heard about?

DOC: Yeah, fourteen of 'em—in the stomach, one a day. (HE *approaches the* PROFESSOR *with a large hypodermic*) Okay, open your shirt.

PROFESSOR: Right now?

DOC: C'mon, open your shirt, man, it's fuckin' hot!

PROFESSOR: Rumor has it these hurt pretty bad.

DOC: I wouldn't know, I've never had one. (*He poises the needle*) Ready?

PROFESSOR (*As* DOC *injects the serum into his abdomen*): No. (*He winces in extreme pain*)

DOC: Rumor's true?

PROFESSOR: Yeah. Well, I can tell ya something burns in there.

DOC: Sit down for a minute, relax. I'm sorry, man. I'm just having a fucked-up day. Sit down for a minute. Relax.

PROFESSOR *(Sits on the book):* Well, here, don't lose your book. *(He holds it out to* DOC*)*

DOC: No, go ahead, you can look at it. Maybe it'll make you feel better.

PROFESSOR: Thanks. You know, this is one of my favorite books.

DOC: You've read that book?

PROFESSOR: Yeah, twice.

DOC: My name's Case. You can call me Doc.

PROFESSOR: My name's Steve, but they all call me the Professor.

DOC: The Professor? Somebody caught you reading a book!?

PROFESSOR: Yeah, that must be it.

DOC: You know what they read around here? On this rack the dude reads *Sports Illustrated.* On the other side of me we've got a dude who reads nothing but *True Detective*— boo-coo fuckin' violence right here in the war. The dude on the next rack jacks off every night to *Wonder Woman* fuckin' comic books!

PROFESSOR: I live in a bunker full of rats, and I'm convinced that they do not read.

78

DOC: You got off easy with the rats, Steve. A couple of weeks ago they brought in a dude with half his ear chewed right off. Un-fuckin' real, man! Sometimes I feel like I'm reading a book about this dude in Vietnam, but it isn't a book—it's real, it's me, and I'm here.

PROFESSOR: I know what you mean. Sometimes I feel like one of Pirandello's characters.

DOC: You know fuckin' Pirandello?

PROFESSOR: Ah, college bullshit.

DOC: Stay right here. I'm gonna get you a beer.

PROFESSOR: You have beer?

DOC: Hey, we're medics. We have everything.

PROFESSOR: So I've heard.

DOC: Oh fuck! Steve, you can't drink beer.

PROFESSOR: The hell I can't!

DOC: No, the treatments, man. Fourteen days—no alcohol.

PROFESSOR: Ah, fuck me!

DOC (*Looks around*): You smoke?

PROFESSOR: Does Pinocchio have a wooden dick?

79

DOC *(Laughs)*: Fuckin' A. Well, I just happen to have . . . *(He produces a handful of joints)* . . . a little numbah-one com sai. *(He lights a joint)*

PROFESSOR: I'm feeling better already.

DOC: Two tokes of this will knock your socks off. *(He takes several long tokes and hands the joint to the PROFESSOR. They share the joint and get stoned during the following dialogue)* I haven't done this in forty-five minutes! Now, rap to me about Pirandello.

PROFESSOR: Now?

DOC: Yeah, man. Talk to me about Pirandello. C'mon, rap to me, Steve, I've got nobody to talk to here.

PROFESSOR: Okay—I always thought his basic premise is that thought has more stability to it than reality, because reality is constantly changing, and because of that, concepts, ideas, things that exist only within the realms of thought, actually have more stability to their reality than the ever-decomposing three-dimensional objects that surround us.

DOC: "The ever-decomposing three-dimensional objects that surround us"! *(Starts hitting hard on the joint)* More, more, Professor!

PROFESSOR: Take Hamlet, for example. From the moment Shakespeare created him down through time, our perception of him hasn't changed, but everything around us changes. Like, six months from now, you and I won't be the same two people we are today.

DOC: Fuckin' A, man! Six months from now this GI will be in a peace demonstration on Nixon's fuckin' front lawn! That's if I can deal with this bullshit for another 157 days.

PROFESSOR: Doc, I got a trick for dealin' with it. You have to learn to escape this country.

DOC: Escaping this country is what we are doing. *(He smokes)*

PROFESSOR: You gotta learn how to totally relax every muscle in your body, and let your thoughts just float away.

DOC: Meditation?

PROFESSOR: Yeah, but no matter how bizarre or weird your thoughts get, you can't put any chains on them. Like the other night, on perimeter guard duty—I vividly imagined all these opera characters, big Wagnerian opera characters. Here, get this picture. *(He gets up and takes the stage)* Over here we have Freia and Fricka. Over here is Fasolt and Fafner, the giants. And then down here is Brünhilde weighing in at four thousand pounds, wearing this helmet of gold and silver . . .

DOC: With big fuckin' horns!

PROFESSOR: Yeah, right! You know these characters. And then we got Wotan, King of the Gods, looking out over everything. They're all naked, running toward one another. And when they meet in the middle, they explode in this spectacular fireworks display! It was like a napalm explosion. Now, I have no idea where a vision that ridiculous came from, but it helped me to get away for just that long! *(He sits back down with* DOC*)*

DOC: Steve, I am here to tell you, that is not meditation. You were totally, absolutely, one hundred percent fuckin' stoned, man. You were stoned!

PROFESSOR: Yeah, you know I never smoked dope before I came to this green suck.

DOC: I bet you never killed anyone before you came to this green suck, either. *(Pause)* Aw, fuck, fuck, fuck it, man! Steve, tell me something. Do you think that God is watching all the shit that's goin' down here?

PROFESSOR: You mean you believe in God?

DOC: Well, I believe in the Buddhist concept. Like God is everywhere, man. He's inside of everything. It's like Hesse says in *Sidhartha*, man. It's as if Buddha is hiding in every round.

PROFESSOR: Oh yeah. Well then, tell me this. If that's true, if there really is some omniscient, superior-intelligent being with supposed control over the whole universe . . .

DOC: God!

PROFESSOR: . . . then why would he create us with a natural desire to kill each other?

DOC: Let's not talk about fuckin' war, okay? It's a downer, man.

PROFESSOR: There's a fuckin' rat! *(He takes* DOC'S *.45 pistol, aims it, pulls the trigger, and it clicks)* Load this motherfucker!

DOC: Hey, man, I don't load it anymore. *(Takes pistol from him)* It's a furry little creature.

PROFESSOR: Why did God create rats?

DOC: Oh, now there's an important religious question we can discuss. Rats are big, ugly, obnoxious, frothing at the mouth, disease-ridden, flea-bitten, rabid . . .

PROFESSOR *(Starts to laugh)*: Okay, okay, I got my high back. *(Pause)* Guard duty! I've got guard duty!

DOC: Reality!

PROFESSOR: I've got to get some coffee and straighten out.

DOC: Yeah, lots of opera characters waiting for you out there. It was nice meeting you, man. We'll rap again. Don't think too much, it'll make you depressed. Ah, the shots, don't miss a day on the shots. If you miss one day, it's back to day one.

PROFESSOR: Pleasant thought!

DOC: Oh, and no alcohol. Smoke dope!

PROFESSOR: All right, I'll see you tomorrow.

DOC: Fuckin' A. Peace.

(Lights cross-fade. Light slowly fades on DOC *during the following monologue)*

PROFESSOR: Well, I went back to see Doc for the thirteen days for the thirteen rabies shots. And I continued to go back for a month or so afterward. Doc and I talked about a lot of things. We became close. We became "tight." Then one night I went to see Doc and I was told that earlier that same evening Doc had taken a .45 and put it to his head. *(Light blacks out on* DOC *at this point)* All that was left was a note. I didn't read the damn note. I remember thinking, I can't converse with a note, I can't relate to a fuckin' note, I can't be friends with a note. And then I sat down and tried to cry. But, as hard as I tried, I could not shed one tear for my friend who had just killed himself. I guess the machine just refused to shut itself off.

(Lights up on the entire stage)

The Machine

WILLIAMS *(Offstage)*: Bury your dicks in the dirt, maggots!

(Four others run onstage in civvies. The five—including the PROFESSOR—*lie face down on the floor)*

WILLIAMS *(Now onstage)*: Elbows and toes, ladies! *(They comply)* You think just 'cause one maggot fucked up, the rest of you are gonna skate? Well, guess again, maggots. In the bush one maggot fucks up, his whole fuckin' platoon gets wasted. On your feet! Move! *(They comply)* Bends and motherfuckers—cadence count—one hundred repetitions. Ready. Exercise.

(The five begin doing squat thrusts, counting off)

ALL: One two three, one, sir. One two three, two, sir. One two three, three, sir.

(They continue exercising as the PROFESSOR addresses the audience, but do not count aloud during the following speech)

PROFESSOR *(Still exercising)*: The machine was a defense mechanism I dreamed up in boot camp. When things got tough, I would just turn my mind off and become a machine. That way, no matter what they threw at us, no matter how hard it got, they could not break my machine. All I had to do was throw a switch.

ALL: One two three, twenty-one, sir. One two three, twenty-two, sir.

WILLIAMS *(Offstage)*: *I . . . can't . . . hear . . . you!!!*

ALL: One two three, twenty-three, sir.

Fuckin' A, We Like It Here

Loud music—"I Want to Take You Higher" by Sly and the Family Stone—cuts in. We are back in 'Nam with the ensemble giving HABU a short-timer's party. We are in the middle of a rowdy, drunken, macho dance. The dance is open to improvisation. In the New York production, DINKY DAU *juggled grenades, there was a chicken fight,* HABU *played tambourine and sang along. The dance improvisation culminates in doing the limbo with an M–16. It's very competitive, with* DINKY DAU *going last. As he goes under the rifle,* SCOOTER *and* BABY SAN *spray beer all over him. A fight ensues between* SCOOTER *and* DINKY DAU. LITTLE JOHN *and* BABY SAN *break it up.* DINKY DAU *turns off the stereo. The music cuts out.*

DINKY DAU *(To* SCOOTER*):* Fuckin' jack-off face!

SCOOTER: Butt—maggot—asshole!

BABY SAN: You fuckin' babies!

HABU: Peace. Peace.

LITTLE JOHN: Next son-of-a-bitch starts a fight, starts it with me.

*(*SCOOTER *goes for him, but immediately backs down)*

HABU: You're all spoilin' my party. Peace.

LITTLE JOHN: Scooter, come here. Dinky Dau, come here. Okay. Work it out.

*(*SCOOTER *and* DINKY DAU *meet in center.* SCOOTER *sprays beer at* DINKY DAU. DINKY DAU *spits beer at* SCOOTER. *They laugh. The beer gets sprayed on* LITTLE JOHN. DINKY DAU *quickly gets a towel to dry him off)*

DINKY DAU: Sorry, Little John.

PROFESSOR: Habu, answer us one question. If you're not going to write, would you let us know now, so we don't fuckin' wait once again for some card or letter that ain't gonna show up! You remember Falcon was gonna write. Owens was gonna write. Hey, Falcon, as I remember, was going to send us a picture of his wife!

DINKY DAU: That's right . . . *naked*!

PROFESSOR: The point is, not one fuckin' GI that's gone back to the world has written us back.

DINKY DAU: You know what it is? You wanna know what the point is? Whenever a GI gets back to the world, the war is over for them. They naturally forget about us guys back in 'Nam.

SCOOTER: The reason he ain't gonna write is, he knows half of us gonna get blown away.

DINKY DAU: Oh, man, you always turn everything into a bummer!

BABY SAN: Fuckin' bummer, Scooter. Fuckin' bummer!

(Pause. The mood sinks)

HABU *(Crosses to center and raises a can of beer)*: Here's to all the guys that missed the "Freedom Bird."

87

(Everyone else follows suit. A ritualistic toast to the dead. Silence. LITTLE JOHN *starts to sing "We Like It Here," to the tune of "O Tannenbaum." Eventually all but the* PROFESSOR *join in. It's a drunken GI song)*

ALL: We like it here. We like it here.
You're fuckin' A, we like it here.

We shine our boots, we shine our brass,
to keep the lifers off our ass.
And even though we got malaria,
we'll still police the fuckin' area.

We like it here. We like it here.
You're fuckin' A, we like it here.

We'll patrol the paddies, sweep the hills,
and triple reports of all our kills.
And even though we got rounds comin' in,
we'll try to suck our bellies in.

We like it here. We like it here.
You're fuckin' A, we like it here.

We'll all be grunts until we're gone,
and say goodbye to Charlie Cong.

We like it here. We like it here.
You're fuckin' A, we like it here.
We like it here. We like it here.
You're fuckin' A, we like it here!

HABU: Short, short, short, short, short, short, short! I'm nine fuckin' days short!

BABY SAN: So what? I've been short all my life.

HABU: What's a few inches, when your spirit's as tall as yours? Baby San, you keep that brass polished.

BABY SAN: I'm going home next, man. I'm going to miss you, man. Keep your nose clean and your ass wiped. And you wipe the floor, Dinky Dau.

DINKY DAU: Fuck you, man.

BABY SAN: I love you, too, man. *(Exits)*

HABU: Little John, you're the spirit here now. You bring 'em on home alive.

(HABU *and* LITTLE JOHN *embrace.* LITTLE JOHN *exits. The* PROFESSOR *stands not too steadily. He waves to* HABU *and exits)*

SCOOTER: Hey, man. 'Nam is home for me, and you're closer than blood. But we won't hang out in the world, 'cause there you'll be black and I'll be white.

HABU: Fuck all that, man. All my maggots is green. And if you ain't green, you're red. And if you're red, you're dead. Goin' to miss you, Scooter.

SCOOTER: You're going to catch the "Freedom Bird." I can't leave, I just extended six months. *(Exits)*

DINKY DAU: Guard duty! I got fuckin' guard duty. *(He starts to exit)* Habu, I've got one last surprise for your fuckin' going-home party. *(He crosses to platform and pulls down his pants)* This is the last moon you'll ever have to sleep under in the fuckin' 'Nam.

HABU: Dinky Dau, you're a crazy motherfucker. As crazy as you is, you got to come home alive.

DINKY DAU: Habu! *(They toast. He exits)*

HABU *(Alone, quietly):* "We like it here. We like it here. You're fuckin' A, we like it here."

1984 Tracers

Bruce Springsteen's "Born in the U.S.A." comes in loud and hard and fades in and out to underscore the following monologues. The actors are spotlighted as in the "The First Tracers," but change to 1980s clothing.

PROFESSOR: November 11, 1984. I was meditating in a Buddhist temple in Bangkok. I was trying to figure out what had brought me back to Southeast Asia. A very young Thai girl sat next to me. I started to speak to her, but nothing came. "What's bothering you?" she asked. I said, "I fought in the Vietnam War." She smiled and said, "Don't think too much. It will make you depressed." I said, "I keep thinking about killing people." She brushed my cheek with her fingertips, and she whispered a sweet and gentle truth: "The war is over. It's time to go home." *(Exits)*

(Music up. Lights cross-fade)

LITTLE JOHN: I was a good soldier and a good citizen. I took orders and had respect for my superiors. Hell, I was just doing my duty. Now I got my little sheet-metal business.

I pay my own way. I pay all my hospital bills. I never beg for anything. My doc says my cancer's running faster now than I am. I won't live past forty. But my little girls will be here. Mary was born without a stomach and Debbie only has one foot. The war drags on. Fuck the VA! Fuck the Agent Orange lawsuit! Fuck Dow Chemical! Fuck the government! *(Exiting)* Fuck it, man! Fuck it!

(Music up. Lights cross-fade)

BABY SAN: My apartment in Manhattan overlooks the Hudson. It's a beautiful seaway. Let's see now, I've traveled the Baltic, the Bosporous, the Mediterranean . . . Cao Dai temples, and South China seas. As a matter of fact, the name of my club is the South China Seas; pretty, huh? We serve a cooling peppermint schnapps over ice, with little paper umbrellas. My pop is very proud of me. Well, I bought him a condo in Miami—I have a club there, too. Married? Not me. I don't know, really, I never keep the same set of friends for too long. I'm pretty much on the go. I think of Saigon from time to time. I did have a party, and somehow I want to say that it was a good time. And I wonder if the only thing I left was a piece of myself. Amerasian children, that's what they call them. *(Exits)*

(Music up. Lights cross-fade)

HABU: I got out for a while. Man, I couldn't hack it. I mean, civilians don't know; hell, they don't even know how to stand in line, man. So, I re-upped, and then I extended. They just gave me my fifth hash mark and my fourth undetected-crime ribbon. I guess I'm just a lonely, ignorant fool evading reality . . . Lifer, lifer, lifer. They've cut the squads down from fourteen men to thirteen now. Things haven't changed much. The kids they send us are a lot like we were. In Lebanon they wouldn't let us have ammo, 'cause we didn't know how to use it and they were afraid we might shoot somebody. Really, man, we're still not giving 'em the training they need. Still, the unwilling led by the uneducated to do the impossible for the ungrateful. Underpaid, underfed, undertrained, overworked, oversexed, highly vulnerable, teenaged targets. But we do our duty. We do our duty. I wonder if they'll build another wall in Washington for the kids in Beirut. *(Exits in military style)*

(Music up. Lights cross-fade)

DINKY DAU *(Enters quickly in a wheelchair)*: I was playing darts with my two ex-wives' pictures. It was the Fourth of July. Everyone else was out celebrating. I was freakin' out, man. But I got myself up and out for a six-pack. I hit the street, and the night sky and the colors and the explosions, man, I started going faster and faster and faster . . . and then I flashed incoming! Boooom . . . off the curb and outta my chair. I was lying in the street, and I looked up, and there she was. I said, Hey, I'm a vet, you wanna dance with me? She smiled and reached out to me. Then she looked at my chair, then back at me, and she began to cry. I reached out to her and she took my hand, and we danced. Two boat people meeting in the night, huh? *(Chuckles)* We've been together for six months now. Her name is Mary. She's Vietnamese. *(He exits dancing in wheelchair)*

(Music up. Lights cross-fade)

SCOOTER: After I got out of prison I went to the Wall in Washington. Now I keep having this dream. In my dream, I walk away from the Wall and suddenly I'm in Vietnam. I board a C–130 in Khe Sanh. I'm on my way to Da Nang for R&R. The plane is filled with body bags. There's no place to sit but on the bags. I'm sitting there and I start to look at the name tags. I recognize some of the names from my childhood. The plane begins to descend. I look down and it's not Vietnam. It's my hometown. I look back and the bags are starting to move. I start freaking out. I jump off the plane before it stops taxiing. But I can't run. I look back and see the bags opening. And one by one, every boy from my high-school graduating class gets out. I feel very calm. I join them and we all walk into town. There is a brass band and a ticker-tape parade. I have no fear. We've all come home—together.

(Surreal light change. The following two scenes are staged in a dreamlike way)

Ambush

Lights up. SCOOTER *is changing to fatigues. We are jolted back to 'Nam.* LITTLE JOHN *enters, takes an M–16 from rack, begins to check it out.*

SCOOTER: Did you get the word yet?

LITTLE JOHN: What? Did they call it off?

SCOOTER: They did?

LITTLE JOHN: I dunno . . . did they?

SCOOTER: I thought you knew.

LITTLE JOHN: Fuck, I don't know shit. Habu come in the hootch screamin' for everyone to get their gear together and muster on the LZ. That's all I fuckin' know.

SCOOTER: Yeah, but did he say where we're going?

LITTLE JOHN: I told you, I don't know shit.

SCOOTER: You know what I heard? I heard Delta Company got their asses totally wiped out—like totally massacred— and we're gettin' sent in to replace them.

LITTLE JOHN: Where'd you hear that?

SCOOTER: That's all they're talkin' about down at the Commo bunker.

DINKY DAU *(Enters)*: Oh fuck! We're in a world of shit now! You guys hear where they're sending us? . . . The DM-fuckin'-Z, motherfuckers. Can you fuckin' believe that?

LITTLE JOHN: Where'd you hear that shit?

DINKY DAU: Couple guys down at the Commo bunker overheard it. The shit is gettin' *heavy* up there, man. You know what I heard? That the NVA are making airmobile assaults in Russian-built helicopters. They're kickin' ass all over I Corps.

SCOOTER: NVA *helicopters!*

DINKY DAU: Goodbye, conflict. Hello, World War III. This ain't no conflict anymore, man. This shit's escalating.

PROFESSOR *(Enters)*: Dinky Dau, what the fuck are you talkin' about? They're just sending us over to Lai Khe to support some ARVNs.

SCOOTER: I thought Delta Company got massacred?

PROFESSOR: They did—First of the Twelfth is going in to support them. Surely you heard that, too.

LITTLE JOHN *(Disdainful)*: Fuck, we're goin' in to support the fuckin' ARVNs?

SCOOTER: Well, fuck the ARVNs.

DINKY DAU: Let the ARVNs fight their own shit. I'm gettin' tired of goin' in for those candy-ass gooks every goddamn time.

BABY SAN *(Shouting offstage as he enters)*: Lifers! I hate you lifer motherfuckers! *(He enters angrily)* Can you fuckin' believe that lifer Williams! I got thirty-three days left in-country and you know where he's sending me?

PROFESSOR: I can't wait to hear!

BABY SAN: Cam-fuckin'-bodia!

SCOOTER: How the fuck can he send you to Cambodia?

BABY SAN: Didn't you guys get the word? That's where the choppers are taking us. The NVA are comin' across the border in Russian-built *tanks*.

LITTLE JOHN: Baby San, c'mon, he's just fuckin' with your head.

BABY SAN: No, he's serious. I only got thirty-three fuckin' days left . . . Williams wants to see me dead.

LITTLE JOHN: Williams may want to see you dead, but not in Cam-fuckin'-bodia.

DINKY DAU: Little John, what did I tell you guys, this shit is *escalating*.

(All argue)

HABU *(Rushes in yelling)*: Clear the LZ! Clear the LZ!

SCOOTER: Let's ask Habu.

(They hurriedly move aside as HABU guides in the chopper. Lights change for chopper effect)

SCOOTER: What's this about us goin' to Cambodia, Habu?

HABU: What?!

DINKY DAU: We all heard! That's the last word that's been goin' around.

HABU: Well, if that's the last word you heard, Dinky Dau, then it must be correct. Let's get ready!

SCOOTER: So where are they takin' us?

HABU: Do you see GENERAL WESTMORELAND written on this shirt? I'm just a fuckin' squad leader—you think they tell me anything?! Get ready to saddle up.

BABY SAN: Habu, I only got thirty-three days left in-country.

HABU: Let's get on that bird! Move!

(All start to move toward chopper)

BABY SAN: Hey, Habu. The only reason Williams is makin' me go out is because he wants me to die!

HABU: Baby San, get your short ass on that bird!

BABY SAN: I've been on enough fuckin' missions, god-damnit! I only got thirty-three days! You're my fuckin' squad leader!

HABU: Get on the fuckin' bird, and I ain't bullshittin' around!

BABY SAN: Fuck it!

(BABY SAN starts swinging at HABU. A scuffle begins. The others pull them apart. All start to slowly board the chopper. Music and sound effects: "Gimme Shelter" by the Rolling Stones mixed with chopper noise)

HABU: Load him on that chopper!

DINKY DAU *(To* BABY SAN*)*: We all have to go, Baby San.

(All board the chopper)

HABU: I need this shit!

(Music up with loud sound effects of chopper lifting off. The actors are talking during lift-off. Sound and music fade)

PROFESSOR: Attitude check!

ALL: *Fuck it!*

LITTLE JOHN: Sit your ass in here, Scooter—you're about to fall out.

SCOOTER: I'm just tryin' to make sure I can jump outta the chopper soon as it lands.

LITTLE JOHN: Well, you best worry about stayin' *inside* of it till we hit the LZ.

*(*SCOOTER *scrunches up his body, places his hands under his crotch)*

LITTLE JOHN *(Amused)*: What are you doin' now, Scooter?

SCOOTER: Just tryin' to protect the family jewels.

LITTLE JOHN: Like *that*?

DINKY DAU: What jewels? You ain't got no fuckin' jewels.

98

SCOOTER: Look who's talkin,' the company eunuch!

DINKY DAU: Professor, what's a eunuch?

PROFESSOR: I swear I'm gonna buy this company a dictionary.

LITTLE JOHN: Means you don't have any balls, Dinky Dau.

PROFESSOR: Give the man a bronze star!

HABU (*Pointing*): Look at that fixed wing goin' in. (*All turn to observe*)

PROFESSOR: Hey, that's heavy shit, man.

SCOOTER: Jesus Christ, Habu, what the hell's goin' on down there?

HABU: Shit's really hittin' it for somebody.

BABY SAN: Hey, is that where we're goin?!

DINKY DAU: Blow the fuck outta 'em.

LITTLE JOHN: They're blowin' the fuck outta somebody.

HABU: Look at them cobras work out.

BABY SAN: Habu, they don't expect us to land right in the middle of that shit?!

HABU: Baby San, shut the fuck up! You're not the only short-timer on this bird!

99

BABY SAN: When I get back, I'm gonna frag that fuckin' Williams.

PROFESSOR: Fraggin' Williams is the best idea I've heard. Just don't get caught.

BABY SAN: What are they gonna do, send me to Vietnam?

SCOOTER: Hey, knock it off, you guys.

(All go silent for a few beats. Music and sound effects swell. All check gear, make sign of the cross, etc. All start to psyche up)

HABU: Red smoke!!! We're goin' in!

PROFESSOR: Why don't they tell us when they're sending us into shit this heavy?

(Music cross-fades to sound effects of a horrendous fire fight. All jump to the landing zone. Lights indicate explosions. The stage is filled with smoke. All leap out of the chopper. Crouching low, they begin darting back and forth in a haphazard manner. All shout frantically)

ALL: Where's the firing comin' from?
Anybody know what the fuck's goin' on?
Who's doin' the shooting?
What direction we supposed to be goin' in?
Movement in the treeline!

HABU: Form up! Skirmish line!

(All except SCOOTER *get blown away, with* BABY SAN *killing himself.* DINKY DAU *is still alive, screaming)*

DINKY DAU: My legs! Scooter, I can't feel my legs!

SCOOTER *(Dazed, he gets to his knees)*: What the fuck? . . . What the fuck? . . . *(He shakes* LITTLE JOHN, *who is dead)* Little John, what the fuck happened?

DINKY DAU *(Moaning)*: My legs . . . I can't feel my legs!

SCOOTER *(Scrambles to* DINKY DAU*)*: Fuck, what's goin' on? Anybody know what happened. *(He is frantic)* Medic! Medic!

DINKY DAU: Are my legs okay, Scooter? I can't feel my legs!

SCOOTER: I'm gonna get a medic. You'll be okay, Dinky Dau. *(Screams) Medic!!* Who's shootin'? Fuck, somebody's still shootin'. Where's my rifle? *(He gets it, but it doesn't work—he throws it aside)* Fuckin' M–16! Gotta keep it together. Be cool, Scooter, be cool. Gotta keep your sanity, man. Christ, what happened to my mind? *(He pulls out a battle dressing and frantically wraps his hand. Suddenly he notices his leg)* Oh no! Oh, Christ! *(Presses down on his leg)* Bleedin' all over the place! Pressure points? Oh, fuck it! *(He begins picking up chunks of dirt and pressing them down into the wound)* Press some dirt down on top of 'em. That oughta stop 'em. Stop bleedin', you motherfucker! Stop! Fuckin' stop! *(Calms himself down)* Keep it together, keep it together. Don't want to go into shock. Most guys die of shock— that's what they taught us. Gotta keep it together. Gotta make a tourniquet. Still bleedin' like crazy. Gotta find a belt . . . tie it off. *(Begins crawling around)* I could still die— lose too much blood. God, I don't wanna die. I don't wanna die here. *(Looks to heaven)* You hear that? I don't wanna die! *(To himself)* Keep it together. Keep it together. Talkin' to God now. Keep your fuckin' sanity, GI! *(Crawls to BABY SAN)* Baby San, Baby San, I gotta tie off my fuckin' leg. Baby San, you fucker. You fuckin' killed yourself.

DINKY DAU: Scooter! Get it together, man! Get me a fuckin' medic!

SCOOTER: Medic! Medic! Medic! Please, God, I need a medic! *(Heavenward)* Please, God, don't let 'em die. Don't let everybody die here. Talkin' to God. I need a medic! *(He aims an M–16 at the sky)* I hate you, God! You hear me?! I hate you! You motherfucker! *(He curls into fetus position and screams "Mama, Mama" over rising music)*

(Lights cross-fade)

The Resurrection (The Ghost Dance)

A ritualistic choreography to raise the dead and pay tribute to the 59,000 who were killed in Vietnam.

Music "Born Never Asked" by Laurie Anderson.

Lighting is dreamlike.

The actors rise slowly and put their weapons away. All face upstage. All turn out at the same time and step through imaginary doors. The upstage curtain slowly lowers to reveal an interpretation of the Vietnam Memorial in Washington ("the Wall"). The actors step forward and slowly salute.

WILLIAMS *appears (apart from the ensemble) and slowly performs a twenty-one-gun salute. The ensemble salutes again. They evolve into a group movement, using Tai Chi forms. The group movement ends with each actor in tableau with some relationship to the Wall, i.e., touching names, looking away, etc.*

Music fades.

Lights cross-fade to general stage light.

The tableau is broken when the PROFESSOR *speaks the first line of the Epilogue.*

Epilogue

The actors deliver the following lines to one another, speaking them simply.

ENSEMBLE: Someone told me you're a vet.
Someone told me you had a gun.
You killed people?
You were only nineteen?
You volunteered?
You're bullshitting me.

Oh, you're one of the lucky ones who made it
   back.

I'm sorry.

I suppose you don't want to talk about it?

Yeah, we saw that on TV.

How was the heat?

How was the rain?

How were the women?

How was Bob Hope?

How does it feel to kill somebody?

You were a pawn.

You were a hero.

You were stupid, you should have gone to
   Canada.

You were there?

You were there?

You were there?

You were there?

You were there?

You were there?

*(Evolve to percussion-based tribal rock chant. It is hard and loud,
a celebration of survival, with sardonic subtext)*

ENSEMBLE: Someone told me you're a vet.

Someone told me you had a gun.

You killed people?

You were only nineteen?

You volunteered?

You're bullshitting me.

Oh, you're one of the lucky ones who made it
   back.

I'm sorry. I'm so so sorry—

I suppose you don't want to talk about it?
Yeah, we saw that on TV.
How was the heat?
How was the rain?
How were the women?
How was Bob Hope?
How does it feel to kill somebody?

(Music grows fainter, then louder again)

You were a pawn.
You were a hero.
You were stupid, you should have gone to
    Canada.
You were there?
You were there?
You were there?
You were there?
You were there?
You were there?
How does it feel to kill somebody?
How does it feel to kill somebody?
How does it feel to kill somebody?

(Blackout)